NONPROFIT ESSENTIALS
Major Gifts

NONPROFIT ESSENTIALS
Major Gifts

Julia Ingraham Walker

WILEY

John Wiley & Sons, Inc.

For general information on our other products and services, or technical support, please contact our Customer Care Department within the United States at 800-762-2974, outside the United States at 317-572-3993 or fax 317-572-4002.

Wiley also publishes its books in a variety of electronic formats. Some content that appears in print may not be available in electronic books.

For more information about Wiley products, visit our Web site at http://www.wiley.com.

Library of Congress Cataloging in Publication Data

ISBN-13 978-0-471-73837-4

ISBN-10 0-471-73837-9

Printed in the United States of America

10 9 8 7 6 5 4 3 2

This book is dedicated to those hundreds of thousands, perhaps millions, of caring individuals who opened their hearts to the victims of Hurricane Katrina. If there was ever a time when philanthropic actions toward others (often unknown and unnamed others) defined the American character, the hurricanes of 2005 and their aftermath proved to be that moment.

The AFP Fund Development Series

The AFP Fund Development Series is intended to provide fund development professionals and volunteers, including board members (and others interested in the nonprofit sector), with top-quality publications that help advance philanthropy as voluntary action for the public good. Our goal is to provide practical, timely guidance and information on fundraising, charitable giving, and related subjects. The Association of Fundraising Professionals (AFP) and Wiley each bring to this innovative collaboration unique and important resources that result in a whole greater than the sum of its parts. For information on other books in the series, please visit:

http://www.afpnet.org

The Association of Fundraising Professionals

The Association of Fundraising Professionals (AFP) represents 26,000 members in more than 170 chapters throughout the world, working to advance philanthropy through advocacy, research, education, and certification programs. The association fosters development and growth of fundraising professionals and promotes high ethical standards in the fundraising profession. For more information or to join the world's largest association of fundraising professionals, visit: *http://www.afpnet.org.*

2005–2006 AFP Publishing Advisory Committee

Linda L. Chew, CFRE, Chair
Associate Director, Alta Bates Summit Foundation

Nina P. Berkheiser, CFRE
Director of Development, SPCA Tampa Bay

D. C. Dreger, ACFRE
Senior Campaign Director, Custom Development Solutions (CDS)

Samuel N. Gough, CFRE
Principal, The AFRAM Group

Audrey P. Kintzi, ACFRE
Chief Advancement Officer, Girl Scout Council, St. Croix Valley

Robert Mueller, CFRE
Vice President, Hospice Foundation of Louisville

Maria Elena Noriega
Director, Noriega Malo & Associates

Leslie E. Weir, MA, ACFRE
Director of Gift Planning, Health Sciences Centre Foundation

Sharon R. Will, CFRE
Director of Development, South Wind Hospice

John Wiley & Sons, Inc.

Susan McDermott
Senior Editor (Professional/Trade Division), John Wiley & Sons, Inc.

AFP Staff

Jan Alfieri
Manager, New Product Development

Walter Sczudlo
Executive Vice President & General Counsel

Acknowledgments

I would like to thank my patient family, along with Jan Alfieri of AFP, Susan McDermott, Kerstin Nasdeo, and all the helpful people at John Wiley & Sons, Inc. for their support when things got tough. Between accidents, hurricanes, and living in exile, the past year has been a challenge. Thanks to all of you for being there.

About the Author

Julia Ingraham Walker holds a BA and MA in English from Tulane University in New Orleans and an MBA from Rollins College in Florida. Her initial marketing expertise was formed during 10 years as a professional in college admissions, first at Tulane and then as director of admissions at Rollins. In 1985 she returned to New Orleans and began a career in fundraising that has spanned 20 years and numerous positions ranging from annual fund to major gifts.

In 1990, Ms. Walker was appointed vice president for institutional advancement at her alma mater, Tulane, where she served until 1998. In this position she supervised over 100 employees in the advancement area and directed the university's $250 million capital campaign. Tulane's campaign raised over $75 million for endowment as well as providing the resources for construction or major renovation of eight campus buildings. In 1994, Ms. Walker was named Outstanding Fundraising Executive by her peers in the New Orleans chapter of the Association of Fundraising Professionals (AFP).

Ms. Walker has been active as an independent fundraising consultant since 1998 and has conducted and advised campaigns that total over $600 million. Her clients include a wide range of nonprofits, from museums and schools to grassroots community organizations. She has helped to manage capital campaigns for clients in religion, healthcare, the arts, historic preservation, low-income housing, K–12 education, universities, and research. Her areas of expertise include campaign feasibility studies, campaign planning and implementation, and nonprofit management, including management and training of nonprofit staff, volunteers, and boards.

Recently Ms. Walker has faced some new challenges in the advancement enterprise through helping nonprofits in the Gulf South recover from the devastation of Hurricane Katrina.

Ms. Walker is a member of AFP and has participated in numerous conferences and workshops on fundraising topics. The mother of two sons, Jacob and Benjamin, Ms. Walker is married to Cedric Walker, a professor of biomedical engineering at Tulane University.

Contents

Introduction

Make no little plans; they have no magic to stir men's blood and probably themselves will not be realized.

—Daniel Hudson Burnham

Last year *The Wall Street Journal* began a weekly column in its Friday *Weekend Journal* section called "Giving Back." Each week the columnist, Elizabeth Bernstein, profiles one donor, the person's major gift, and tells briefly how it came about. Many of the gifts profiled are huge—ranging from $1 million to over $100 million—and they are made in support of organizations that do work in a wide range of fields, from science research to housing for the homeless. A novice in the field of major gifts could do a lot worse than reading Ms. Bernstein's column every week to gain a better understanding of why donors make major gifts.

But why does the *Journal*, the newspaper of record in the world of business, devote space and time to major gifts? There is, of course, always that nosy interest we all secretly have in the lifestyles of the rich and the famous, and some of the donors profiled are definitely household names. More commonly, however, the donors selected are successful businesspeople, people who have made lots of money, and the *Journal* is definitely about making money.

Now, however, it has become big news when people give away big money. We all want to know: Why are they making this gift? Who will get the money? How will it be used? Why this nonprofit, and not that one? The tale of wealth in America has segued into a story of philanthropic intent; it has moved from how people made their money to how they are giving it away.

After working with thousands of major donors, I believe that people give because they want to see something good happen, something they believe in, something that requires their investment to become a reality.

From David Rockefeller (who recently made known $100 million bequests to both Rockefeller University and the Museum of Modern Art in New York) to two navy veterans who gave $1 million to make the *USS Saratoga* into a memorial, the story of major gifts is the story of donors' belief that they can make a meaningful difference in their world, an impact on the lives of others.

This book tells the story behind the giving of the major gift, the story of the volunteers, board leaders, and staff members who build a program compelling enough to attract donors who make large gifts. From strategic planning to prospect research, this book aims to help organizations implement a major gift program that will draw big resources to help fund big ideas.

The best kind of major gift is the one that falls out of a conversation that takes place between the right people, about the right cause, at the right time. Donors of big gifts are not forced or manipulated; they are people who choose to use their resources to make something happen. They are optimists by nature, who think that the individual can effect change in society. Linking your organization's vision of that change to each donor's personal concept of making a difference is the real key to major gifts.

If you want to know what God thinks of money, just look at the people he gave it to.

—Dorothy Parker

CHAPTER 1

Introduction to Major Gifts

After reading this chapter you will be able to:

- Define a major gift for your organization
- Build a prospect-centered program
- Determine your readiness for a major gifts program

What Is a Major Gift?

Major gifts are an essential component of successful nonprofit fundraising programs today. Effective major gift programs raise more money at less cost for an organization's identified needs than any other fundraising programs. Without major gifts, organizations are forced to depend on the lower and less efficient returns of annual fund, direct mail, telemarketing, special events, and online fundraising efforts. It is easy to understand why organizations desire major gifts. But what exactly is a major gift, why do donors make large gifts, and how can an organization prepare to launch a major gifts program?

Some major gifts are instantly recognizable. When a nonprofit announces that a long-term supporter has contributed $1 million to build a new facility, even a casual observer would call that a *major gift*. A gift of $500,000 to establish an endowment to support a pressing need, such as a community health program, would also be easy to define as a major gift. But what about the donor who raises her annual contribution from $500 to $1,000? Or the company that makes a one-time grant of $10,000 to underwrite an event? In order for your organization to create an effective, ongoing program to attract major gifts, you must first define what gifts you will be seeking.

Defining Major Gifts by Size

Probably the simplest way to define a major gift is by size of the gift. It is useful to look at the historical dollar levels of annual gifts made to your organization when setting the entry dollar level for your major gift program. Most organizations count on a large number of small annual gifts, paid within a fiscal year by cash, check, or credit card, to keep their programs running. Study the pattern of these small, regular annual gifts in order to determine the highest level typically given within a normal year by your top group of annual donors. Ignore any unique, large, one-time gifts or grants that skew the regular gift pattern. Then set the entry level for your major gifts program at a dollar level from 5 to 10 times above this "normal" giving cap.

What your organization defines as a major gift needs to fit the circumstances, needs, and historical fundraising performance of your institution. There are organizations that will struggle to find donors who can contribute $1,000; for them, setting a major gift entry level of $25,000 is not a realistic option. Some sophisticated nonprofits, including hospitals and universities that have had major gift programs for years, identify various tiers for their major gift donors, beginning at five-figure levels and going all the way up to seven- and eight-figure gifts (see Exhibit 1.1).

Defining Major Gifts by Purpose

Many major gifts are given for a specific purpose, further distinguishing them from the annual gift, which is usually unrestricted for current operations. Major gifts are likely to be given in a restricted manner to accomplish a specific purpose valued by the donor. Gifts can be solicited for specific purposes, based on both the organization's needs and the donor's stated preferences. Most major gifts are given in order

EXHIBIT 1.1

Defining the Base Level Major Gift

Set the entry-level major gift 5 to 10 times larger than the highest annual gift typically received by your organization.

If Your Highest Level of Annual Gift Is:	Set Your Entry Level for a Major Gift at:
$500	$2,500 to $5,000
$1,000	$5,000 to $10,000
$2,500	$10,000 to $25,000
$5,000	$25,000 to $50,000
$10,000	$50,000 to $100,000
$25,000	$100,000 to $250,000
$100,000	$500,000 to $1,000,000

to further the stated mission and goals of the nonprofit, but it is up to the nonprofit's leadership to determine if a specific gift is appropriate for the organization's needs and future goals.

A major gift can be made for any of these purposes:

- Unrestricted gifts
- Restricted gifts
- Capital gifts
- Programmatic gifts
- Gifts for endowment

Unrestricted Gifts

Unrestricted gifts can be used within the current fiscal year to meet the needs of current operations, such as salaries, ongoing programs, overhead, utilities, maintenance, facility upkeep, and the like, as identified within the organization's budget process.

Restricted Gifts

A restricted gift is a gift where the donor places a restriction on the use of the funds, such as when, where, and how the money can be spent. An organization is legally required to see that the funds are used as the donor requests. It is incumbent on the organization to not accept a restricted gift if the leadership feels that it cannot, or will not, use the funds as restricted by the donor.

Capital Gifts

Capital gifts are restricted by the donor for use in a specific capital project, usually in response to the stated need of the organization, such as construction of a new facility, renovating a facility, buying land, or other one-time capital outlay.

Programmatic Gifts

Programmatic gifts are restricted by the donor to initiate or support ongoing programs that serve the mission of the organization, such as educational outreach, or to provide specific services, such as delivery of food to the homeless.

Gifts for Endowment

Endowment gifts are those wherein the principal gift amount is invested and preserved, and only the interest income is spent on a purpose identified by the donor. Endowed gifts may be unrestricted or restricted in purpose, depending on the donor's stated desires.

Note: It is the donor, not the nonprofit, who determines the use of a gift.

Nonprofits are not required to accept gifts for a purpose they do not intend to honor, and in practice most major gifts are negotiated agreements between the donor and the nonprofit's executive or board leadership. An organization can work with the donor to specify the use that it desires for major gifts, or it can solicit major gifts for a specific purpose. For instance, a nonprofit board might decide that it wishes to start a new program to underwrite a community initiative that requires programmatic funds, and it can solicit major gifts that are restricted in support of this program. These restrictions, or the terms of the donation, are best worked out with the donor in advance of the contribution and preserved in writing to prevent future misunderstandings.

Types of Major Gifts

Your organization also will need to define gift policy for acceptance of certain types of larger gifts. Although some major gifts come in the form of a check for all the money at one time, it is much more common to have donors pledge large gifts over a period of time. Many major gift donors also consider some type of planned giving arrangement either to preserve a tax advantage or to meet an estate planning goal when giving away large sums of money or other assets. It is useful for the organization to review and define its policies in these areas when starting a major gift program.

Outright Gifts

Cash or checks that cover the gift amount in full are the easiest form for a nonprofit to accept a major gift, but these outright gifts don't always meet the donor's needs.

Pledges

The most common way in which donors pay off a major gift is through pledges. Most organizations set a time limit on pledges of from three to five years, depending on their financial situation and the cash flow needs of the project being supported by the pledge. Pledges of 10 years and longer are sometimes offered, however, so your organization needs to decide whether this is an acceptable way for you to receive the funds.

Remember to get any pledge agreement and timetable in writing and keep it in your files to avoid future misunderstandings. Often the people who originally negotiated a gift have left the organization by the time a 5- or 10-year pledge is fully paid out.

Gifts of Stock or Other Negotiable Securities

Due to the tax benefits of making a gift of appreciated stock, many donors of major gifts find this a useful way to fulfill their contribution or pledge. Make sure your organization can handle the timely transfer of privately owned stock or other securities and that the financial staff and the advancement staff communicate with each other when these gifts are received and booked.

Planned Gifts

The connection between planned giving and major gifts is an important one that will be discussed more fully in Chapter 8. For now, however, consider whether your

LIVE & LEARN

You're Giving to What?

A wealthy alumnus who had long supported the school's athletic program through annual gifts was being courted for a big gift to the campaign for the athletic facility renovation. After several meetings with the athletic director, he agreed to a $500,000 pledge. The school was thrilled—for a week. He called back to explain sheepishly that when his wife found out, she told him they would only support academic programs. "You know," he said, "our foundation is funded from her side of the family."

Moral of the story: Find out who makes the decisions, and include them in the process.

organization needs to set policies concerning the acceptance and counting of major gifts that are also planned gifts.

Many organizations receive their largest major gifts through bequests. It is not uncommon for a donor who might have supported a nonprofit for years with smaller gifts to make a larger gift in her will or estate plan. There are many ways you can encourage this kind of long-term giving relationship, especially through the positive stewardship of the donor's gifts over many years.

Recognition of Major Gifts

Most organizations announce and recognize major gifts at the time that they are promised in writing, even if the gift involves a pledge over a period of time. (Bequests and other deferred giving arrangements are an exception to this rule; see "Tips & Techniques.") Many organizations are eager to announce large gifts as soon as they are closed, in order to show progress toward major goals, keep the rank-and-file donors motivated, and raise the sights for other potential major gift donors.

Public recognition is the currency of major gift giving in most American nonprofits today. Recognition involves making an agreement, either implicit or explicit, that the donor will receive a certain type of public naming, signage, or other nonmonetary consideration in return for giving a gift of a certain size. Often the recognition offered escalates with the size of the gift. A small number of donors request anonymity, which, ironically, is sometimes harder for an organization's staff to grant than public recognition.

Recognition can be granted through a number of means (see Exhibit 1.2). Your organization can put up signs or plaques to name spaces, such as rooms, labs, computer facilities, offices, conference rooms, gardens, courtyards, buildings, wings, or even an entire campus. These recognition options are most often used during a capital campaign, but they can be awarded at any time for an appropriate-level donation if the organization has unnamed spaces that are attractive to donors.

An institution also can choose to recognize major gift donors through linking the donor's name to programs, dinners, events, or other types of public activities. Often these gifts are viewed as either one-time or ongoing sponsorships and are priced according to the visibility associated with the program or event in the community at large. Some organizations separate the solicitation and recognition of major gifts per se from sponsorships and the purchase of dinner tables at fundraising events; however, as long as you are consistent, you can set whatever policies you and your volunteers desire.

EXHIBIT 1.2

Sample Recognition Chart
(Independent School)

Gift Level	Recognition Awarded
$10,000	One-time program sponsor, listed in annual report
$25,000	Program sponsor for 3 years, listed in annual report
$100,000	Name engraved on wall, named scholarship fund
$250,000	Name engraved on wall, named teaching fund
$500,000	Name engraved on wall, named endowed teaching position
$1,000,000	Name engraved on wall, name on small theater
$5,000,000	Name on signage on exterior of new arts building

Printing the names of donors on lists, annual reports, and programs is another popular method for recognizing major gift donations. It is wise to print any donor lists with a cutoff date to ensure that late donors are not miffed at being left out. Donor walls can be a very attractive option for major gift donors, especially if they are located in a prominent place within the installation and can be easily viewed by guests and visitors.

Major gift donors also respond well to a wide variety of small gifts and benefits that are specially arranged for them. Be careful that your organization isn't spending more than donors give to recognize their gift! Also be sure to follow all IRS rules for informing donors about the cost of gifts that they are receiving; such gifts might have to be subtracted from the amount of the gift that is tax deductible.

Popular examples of gifts and benefits for donors include:

- Engraved plaques

- Special membership benefits

- Commemorative crystal pieces or small sculptures

- Posters and framed prints

- Signed books

- Special behind-the-scenes visits or tours

- Invitations to private lunches or dinners

Some organizations initiate donors above a certain level into formal leadership gift societies, replete with proclamations and medals. Even anonymous donors appreciate being invited to a private dinner with the chair of the board or the

---

 RULES OF THE ROAD

Development counting means learning how to count a gift three times:

1. When it is promised
2. When it is given
3. When it is spent

---

executive director of the nonprofit. In general, if it's in good taste, if it matches the needs of the donor and the organization, and if it is agreed on by all parties, you can recognize a donor in any creative way you wish.

It is important to iron out recognition issues at the front end of the gift, when the gift is being negotiated, and put in writing the agreement between the donor and the institution receiving the gift. This avoids hurt feelings, angry donors, and even lawsuits later on in the lifetime of the gift. Some donors make a contract with an organization outlining the recognition to be awarded. Some organizations prepare a gift agreement, signed by the donor, with the specifics of the gift recognition. Whether your arrangements are formal or informal, make sure to leave records for those who come behind you at your institution.

Prospect-Centered Major Gifts

In order to raise major gifts, the nonprofit organization should focus on creating a *prospect-centered program,* a program that develops the capacity to engage and solicit donors individually, based on each donor's unique interests and needs. Most major gifts are solicited through a face-to-face meeting, in which volunteers and/or staff members of the organization attempt to show how the donor can help the organization. *It is also important to consider how the organization will meet the donor's interests and needs.* To meet those interests and needs, fundraisers need to understand what motivates donors to make lasting contributions through larger gifts (see Exhibit 1.3).

Personal Meaning

With a few exceptions, most donors aren't born, they are created. Of course there are a small number of recognizable family names with third- or fourth-generation wealth, where each new generation is inculcated with the spirit of philanthropy from birth. The norm in America today is that most donors of big gifts give because the cause they are giving to is meaningful to them. Philanthropy could be defined as an investment in a meaningful cause by one who has funds left over after personal (and family) material needs have been met.

Each individual selects the definition of what is a meaningful cause to him or her. It may be political, religious, educational, or health-oriented. It may involve

---

EXHIBIT 1.3

What Motivates Donors to Make Major Gifts?

- Commitment to the nonprofit's mission and goals
- Desire to bring positive change to a community or society
- Religious and personal values
- Interest in setting a good example for others
- Peer pressure and expectations or a request from a peer
- Desire to share one's wealth with others less fortunate
- Public recognition for oneself or family members
- Desire to make a "major impact" in solving an issue or problem
- Tax consequences, estate planning, or financial planning goals
- Family history and upbringing

---

the arts, the homeless, those who can't read, or those with cancer. The world has recently seen a huge outpouring of generosity on behalf of millions of survivors of the Asian tsunamis; closer to home, millions have been raised for Hurricane Katrina relief. Beyond these huge disaster relief efforts, however, most donors tend to give their largest gifts to organizations that promote lasting benefit in their own communities.

Many gifts arise from a sense of religious obligation and are a response to moral teachings to provide help for those who are less fortunate. For example, in the Jewish faith, a core value known as *tzedakah*, or the giving of charity, aid, and assistance to the needy, is considered an obligation for all Jews. All of the major faiths teach the values of compassion and support for those in need. Although Americans give more annually to their religious institutions than to any other type of nonprofit, their decision to give to any organization, religious or otherwise, is almost always aligned with their core personal values.

RULES OF THE ROAD

It takes money to raise money.

A key motivating point for donors who make major gifts is the desire to effect change. In our society, most people believe that one's life and actions can effect change and bring improvement to the lot of others. This feeling of active involvement, of driving change through one's personal commitment, is at the heart of many major donations: *Donors wish to have an impact on solving a problem or issue, in alignment with their personal values, where they feel they can make a difference.*

Opportunities for volunteer involvement and activity can also become a catalyst for major donations. Most nonprofits have become adept at the use of volunteers for a variety of tasks, from serving on the governing board to implementing the services that they provide to meet their mission. Many donors give where they are involved, and if they are involved in more meaningful ways, they may give in more meaningful ways. In some cases the donor of a major gift may want to join the organization's board or play a larger role in how the organization moves forward. This desire may become a benefit or a hindrance to furthering the relationship with the donor, depending on how open and inclusive the organization is willing to be.

The great majority of decisions about large gifts are made with forethought and planning. Few donors just respond off the cuff to a request, no matter how eloquent or moving, for hundreds of thousands of dollars to support a cause. Underlying their decision to make a major gift, donors are making a host of smaller decisions that ultimately will affect their gift to an organization. They are asking themselves questions about the meaning of the gift, the organization's direction, and whether their own goals are aligned with those of the nonprofit.

Aligning the cause you are fundraising for with the values of those you seek to attract gifts from is crucial to developing and maintaining a successful major gifts program. In order to attract the attention and support of donors who wish to make an impact on their world, your organization needs to have a vision and a plan for how

TIPS & TECHNIQUES

Questions a Donor Might Ask When Making a Major Gift

- What is this organization doing that is meaningful to me?

- Can I make an impact by giving to this organization?

- Do I agree with the vision, direction, and goals of this organization?

- Are the people who support this organization the kind of people I want to associate with?

- Are there ways I can get involved in this organization in addition to giving money?

- Is this organization going to make good use of my gift?

- Will my gift be put to work to effect change in the areas I care about?

the work you do will effect change. Providing the donor with the opportunity for meaningful interaction with your organization and the people you serve can be a powerful motivational factor.

Donors and Motivation

Major gift fundraising also involves inherently egocentric rewards, such as donor recognition, naming rights, and ongoing stewardship and attention from the organization. The donor's decision to align with a specific nonprofit, and to make a major investment of funds, is often the product of a combination of factors, ranging from philanthropic to egocentric. Different donors respond to different stimuli. The art of major gift fundraising is to appeal to the right donor with the right opportunity at the right time.

Recognition is the most widely practiced "return on investment" for the major gift donor. Recognition may be private—as in a quiet thank-you dinner with the chair of the organization—or it can mean emblazoning the name of the donor on the front of your building. It all depends on what the donor desires, how much he or she gives, and what the nonprofit has to offer for recognition purposes. Most major donors like to see their name in publications, lists, and engraved on donor walls, especially if it's spelled right. Others, generally in the minority, give anonymously or give with little interest in seeing their name in lights; they may desire privacy, they may not want to be called on by the next organization that needs funds, or they may be genuinely humble.

The public recognition of good works makes many people feel better about themselves. Although this may seem self-serving, there are also other reasons for wanting to make a large gift public. Leaders on a nonprofit board, for instance, often want to set the pace and show other potential donors the generous gifts they have made to promote additional giving. Many donors who make gifts large enough to earn "naming rights" will name something for a deceased family member, such as a child, parent, or other loved one, whose name is thus honored forever through the act of donation. In any case, there are worse ways to earn public approbation than seeking recognition by making a large charitable donation; one could argue that this type of public display furthers the common good.

Peer acceptance and approval also play a role in charitable giving, just as they do in many other social and business practices. Board leaders, for instance, often establish a standard expectation of gift size, either formally or informally, through their own giving levels. In order to be a member of a board's inner circle, many board members will ante up to an informal or "accepted" giving level. Working with the board to help identify the early gifts that set this peer giving level is an important objective for the executive director or advancement vice president.

Sometimes a group mentality develops in major gift giving, when donors wait to see what friends and colleagues are giving to a program before making their own commitment. Reunion gifts within a class at a university follow this kind of pattern, for instance. Some donors, especially those who enjoy a competitive spirit, play a kind of one-upmanship game with each other, trying to top each others' gift levels through a friendly charitable competition. The use of celebrities to make a pitch for a nonprofit organization also can tap into the urge to see and be seen in a project that attracts notice from people who are outstanding or who are exciting to be around.

Peer solicitation, probably the most commonly observed practice in major gifts work, is at its root another method of encouraging donors to do what their peers are doing. Experienced volunteer solicitors tell the prospect the level of their own gift and ask the prospect to match that level or to do something similar. Often, major gifts are solicited by business associates and friends of the prospect for just this reason: It is hard to say no to someone with whom the prospect wants to be considered a social or business equal. Sometimes major gifts are solicited by a peer whom the donor "owes," in the sense of needing to return a favor, or a friend who asked the prospect to give to a favorite nonprofit. The key to the success of the solicitation often is figuring out these kinds of social patterns to get the right solicitor matched to the right donor.

The Role of Money and Timing

Donors of larger gifts also have a variety of financial issues to consider, over and above the personal motivational forces just discussed. Unlike gifts to the annual fund or other small contributions, which often are made by cash or check from the donor's available cash flow, the size and timing of a major gift results from the complex interplay of a variety of financial issues. These issues include factors such as income, assets, and taxes, combined with long-term issues such as estate planning, financial planning, and family attitudes toward money. Getting to know your major gift prospects also means learning to understand their attitudes, values, and plans with regard to their financial situation.

Take the interplay between income and assets, for instance. Most small gifts are made from income; many major gifts, however, are made from the donor's assets. This dependence on asset-based giving is the reason that many major gift professionals also need to become conversant with the basics of planned giving. A donor, no matter how willing, is probably not going to sell his primary home to make a large gift to your organization, but he might sell or gift to you his vacation home. The tax benefits that will accrue to the donor and the selection of the best asset to use to make the gift often make a big difference in increasing the gift size.

Family circumstances, timing, and attitudes toward inheritance will also affect major gift giving. Donors nearing retirement age, for instance, often are concerned about their ability to live on the assets they have accrued during their working years.

Planned giving vehicles, such as charitable gift annuities, bequests, and charitable trusts, are useful tools with donors in these circumstances. Some wealthy older parents feel that their middle-age children have all the financial wherewithal they need and are open to giving accumulated assets to a charitable entity; others find that their children are less secure financially and want to care for family members first.

Organizations may also find that the purpose of a gift varies with the donor's attitudes and interests in financial matters. For example, some major donors are interested in seeing all of their money put to work right away in order to make an immediate impact; they may be better candidates for gifts to support capital projects or educational programs. Other donors, especially those who are investors themselves and who have a feel for long-term investment returns, prefer to make gifts that support the long-term financial health of the nonprofit. These individuals make good donors to the endowment.

Often donors will establish a pattern of giving through all their philanthropic activities. The nonprofit can discern this pattern as part of getting to know donors and their preferences. This is why individualized prospect research is a crucial component of a major gifts program. Prospect research sources, strategies, and skills are discussed further later.

Building a prospect-centered major gifts program means that your organization needs to create a diverse array of options to meet your donors' motivations and needs. Whether these options include public recognition or meaningful volunteer experiences, major gift donors will respond best to a program uniquely tailored to their interests and circumstances. Your knowledge of each of your major gift prospects, including their personal experiences, financial plans, values, and long-term goals, will help to motivate the best possible gift from each individual donor.

Are You Ready for a Major Gifts Program?

It may seem axiomatic that if your organization needs more money, you are ready to raise large gifts. Many institutions find, however, that substantial thought and action is required before they can move ahead with a major gifts program. What will your organization use the money for? Who will do the asking? What will be the role of your board and executive director? How will your organization provide for the budget and staffing of this new initiative? These issues need to be addressed early in the process in order to make your program successful from the start.

Organizational Readiness

A nonprofit can take several steps to get ready for a major gifts initiative. Often an executive director will assume—erroneously—that all the activity needs to take place in the advancement office. Yet there are other aspects of the organization that need to be enhanced before fundraising for major gifts can be successful (see Exhibit 1.4).

Assessing the organization's needs and prioritizing those needs is a basic first step. Building leadership and board involvement is also a key component of major gifts work. Questions about staffing and budget may need to be addressed. Beyond these internal issues, however, the organization needs to show potential donors that it is fiscally responsible, successful in adhering to its mission, and provides the services it says it will provide. No one wants to give hundreds of thousands of dollars to a nonprofit that is in the middle of a major scandal or that hasn't balanced its operating budget for years. "Taking care of business" is a priority for all organizations that wish to attract broad and deep financial support.

EXHIBIT 1.4

Questions to Ask: Is Your Organization Ready for a Major Gift Program?

1. What will your organization accomplish with additional funding?

2. Are your board members ready to give and get major gifts?

3. Do you have the appropriate gift policies and procedures in place?

4. Do you need to hire and train additional staff?

5. Do you have a long-term commitment from your board and executive leadership to see the program to a successful conclusion?

6. Are you committed to running an ethical program?

7. Do you have recognition plans for gifts of different sizes and types?

8. Are your potential solicitors identified, ready, and trained?

Assessing Your Organization's Needs

All organizations have competing needs. Nonprofit leaders and boards often struggle to set priorities for where the money should go when funds are limited: Should more staff be hired? New programs rolled out? Facilities and program delivery improved? What about building the endowment for future needs? Assessing your organization's most pressing needs before beginning a major gift program sometimes can be a contentious and divisive process, but it is a necessary one.

Your organization should have a plan for how it will use more money before you begin asking for it. Don't put the cart before the horse; ideally, your leaders should first set the institutional mission and goals, then create the plan for implementation of those goals, and only at that point solicit gifts to move the implementation process along. Organizations without adequate planning are at risk of being "hijacked," or moved in new directions, sometimes against their will, by a donor who will use money and ideas to determine the direction the institution takes.

Strategic planning—the process of planning where your organization is going and what future paths to select in order to meet your goals—is a useful precursor to major gift fundraising. The planning process can be long and complex or short and focused. A major strategic planning initiative, with input across the organization from many various stakeholders, can be a daunting and time-consuming process. Some planners now feel that the rate of change in economic, cultural, and social terms is accelerating, making a long-term planning horizon for nonprofit services less useful.

As an alternative to a broad planning effort, consider focusing in on a few specific areas of need with time frames that are easily grasped, such as five years or less. Fundraising programs that result from such a focused approach are more likely to appeal to donors than longer-term strategic plans, since they are probably better grounded in reality than vague glimmers of issues that might arise 20 years hence.

It helps to attract new money if the organization appears to be doing well with the money it already brings in. Take a long hard look at the financial health and fiscal management of your organization before beginning your major gift effort. Donors of large gifts are usually pretty savvy about smelling out financial shenanigans or slack accounting practices, and they are perfectly comfortable asking hard questions about budgets, salaries, contracts, and leases.

TIPS & TECHNIQUES

Options for Focused Strategic Planning Efforts

- Create a master facility plan for the next five years; get costs for renovations and new additions. Phase in new projects so that you will have maximum flexibility. Build your fundraising goals around the master plan.

- Determine how much endowment income is needed to ensure the ongoing delivery of current services over the next five years. Develop an endowment goal based on raising the principal needed to ensure this income level.

- Plan to add a new program that can be implemented over the next three years. Establish all costs, including operating budgets, staff, and overhead, with increasing goals over the three-year period. Tie new funding to the desirability of achieving the new program.

- Refocus your mission and goals on a broader regional spectrum rather than serving just a small local audience. Establish a five-year plan for rolling out new and expanded services. Develop a cost estimate that ties additional services and outreach to additional funds.

- Do a national survey of selected peer institutions, requesting information on program development, endowment, budget, and staffing. Use this information to inform your planning efforts.

If, for instance, your organization doesn't manage its accounts aggressively, earning interest on money that isn't being used, donors might well question whether you have earned the right to manage their funds. Investment practices for endowed funds are also a favorite area of intense attention for prospective donors. Your chief financial officer may resent the intrusion, but donors who give big money expect to be kept informed about how "their" money is used. The bottom line is to expect donors to apply the same careful business acumen to a nonprofit's business practices that they have applied to earn (and keep) their own fortunes.

Leadership: A Key Ingredient

Building appropriate leadership and buy-in from the board are important factors in major gifts fundraising. Many experienced professionals view board and volunteer leadership as the key factor for success. First, make sure that your board has approved the budget and policy changes necessary to build a strong major gifts program. If this includes either long- or short-term strategic planning, give the board the time and the necessary data to discuss the implications of the new programs and plans thoroughly. A board member who is sold on the mission of the organization, its executive leadership, and its future plans makes a good donor and a strong addition to the major gifts team.

It is incumbent on those board members who have the financial wherewithal to see the value of making their own major gifts before others in the community are approached. When presented with a proposal for a large contribution, many

IN THE REAL WORLD

Leadership in Major Gifts Fundraising

A university decided to run a five-year national campaign to raise major gifts to fund new initiatives and build its endowment. On a consecutive basis, they asked each of three board members who had the potential to make large gifts to serve as their chair. One after another, the donors declined; one had an ailing family member, another was focused on a different charity, and the last didn't feel comfortable in a position that was so visible.

The school began the campaign anyway, using staff, some volunteers, and the president to raise most of the gifts. Although there was limited initial success, the effort soon floundered as it became clear that many of the expected early large gifts were missing. What to do? Clearly the leadership needed to set the pace, for major gifts were missing.

The advancement staff and the president brainstormed and came up with a solution. They returned to the initial three board members and asked them all to serve together as co-chairs for the drive. With support from the staff, the three agreed to lead the effort, which soon began to build momentum with several new large gifts. After all of the co-chairs committed to a new large gift of their own, the campaign moved quickly toward success.

experienced donors will ask what the board has done to support the effort. Some boards may need to be augmented with new members who can ask for and make large gifts before a major gifts effort is launched. Most boards will need additional training and support from either the advancement staff or an outside consultant to prepare them to take part in a major gifts effort. An organization with a board that sits back and waits for the executive director and the staff to "make it happen" is not going to succeed.

Who Will Ask for Major Gifts for Your Organization?

If the answer is only members of the development staff, your program is already headed for trouble. There is no question that advancement professionals should lead the team effort to raise big gifts. They should direct the research and planning, help to identify prospects, direct the fundraising activity, track the results, work directly with the donors, and provide all the necessary support for volunteers and executive staff who interact with donors. The advancement director and the major gift staff members should be trained and prepared to ask for large gifts. However, often others connected to the organization may be better positioned to ask for and close a big gift.

The person who is most likely to get the gift should be the one who makes the solicitation, whether it is the chair of the board or the program coordinator who has worked with the donor for years. In cases where the right solicitor isn't an obvious choice, a team approach is often the most productive answer.

In many organizations, the person most likely to get the gift is the president or executive director. She is often the best spokesperson for the mission and vision with major donor prospects and may be the most articulate in describing the opportunities for meeting the organization's goals. Her ability, experience, and passion for the cause often help her to convey the needs of the organization in a manner that is truly compelling to the prospective donor.

If the executive director is unable or unwilling to fill this role, training should be provided. Fear or reluctance to do fundraising is a poor excuse; the board should make it a priority to attract executive leaders who can build the organization by raising funds. Many workshops and seminars are now offered at a high level by the Association of Fundraising Professionals (AFP), the Council for Advancement and

Support of Education (CASE), the American Association of Museums (AAM), and other fundraising groups to help train chief executives to become great fundraisers.

Board members and other volunteers can also be provided with training and options for developing additional expertise before a big funding initiative is started. One of the most effective ways to train good fundraising volunteers is to pair them with an experienced major gifts solicitor (either a staff member or an experienced volunteer) and have them make some calls together. The advancement director can take this approach with a reluctant executive director, an inexperienced board member, or a program director who will have substantial donor contact.

The goal is to have an array of solicitors—board members, volunteers, executive directors, advancement staff members, major gift officers—who are ready and willing to work with prospective donors and who are knowledgeable enough to represent the organization in a positive, professional, and productive manner.

Summary

Building a major gifts program from the ground up requires attention to giving policies, strategic planning, and organizational leadership. Take the time to educate and inform your executive director and board about the long-term investments that will be required to make the program work. Begin creating support for future major gifts from your board members and closest supporters with a strategic planning exercise that will help your organization determine what it intends to accomplish with the additional funds raised.

Tailor the program to your leadership by identifying board members who can give or ask for gifts at a high level. Plan to add new board members or provide additional training to current members in order to develop a cadre of volunteers who can help lead the major gifts effort. The executive director should be primed and ready to make building donor relationships an important part of the job. Although the advancement staff will be an integral part of the new effort, they can't succeed without knowledgeable, capable board members, along with the executive leadership, volunteers, and donors to help move the program forward.

CHAPTER 2

Building a Major Gifts Program

After reading this chapter you will be able to:

- Institute the key components of a major gifts program
- Hire, supervise, and train major gift staff members
- Identify and research major gift prospects

Key Components of a Major Gifts Program

Creating a major gifts program from the ground up takes time, money, and focus. It also requires the commitment of the executive director or president and the board, and ongoing support from the entire advancement operation. A strong major gifts program is an important investment in the future of the organization that will pay off in the long run.

Most major gifts require a long lead time between identification of the prospect and closing the gift. It can literally take years to develop the kind of relationship that is required to close gifts of $1 million or more. Because of this lead time, it is important to present a new major gifts program to your board as a long-term investment in the organization.

The Heart of the Program: Major Gifts Staff

Most advancement operations will start with one or two major gifts officers and build a staff from there. A complex organization, such as a multipronged community service organization, might want to assign a major gifts officer to each service area. Universities often hire a major gifts person for each college or program, including the library and athletics. These staff members then report up through a hierarchical system to a dean, a director of major gifts, or a campaign director in the advancement office.

The number of staff and the structure you establish is also related to the amount of money you desire to raise. You will need to assess the maturity of your program and the depth of your donor base. In general, starting a major gifts program from scratch requires more staff and more advance time than keeping one going that has been running for some time. This is because it often takes several years to move from the identification of a donor to the actual closing of a gift from that donor, so programs that have donors "in the pipeline," or who are already being approached and cultivated, can bring in more gifts faster.

Major gift officers develop a rare set of skills, and often they are rewarded for a track record that illustrates their success in applying their skills. These skills include, but are not limited to: relationship building, integrity, familiarity with business and investment terminology, excellent communications skills, willingness to travel and to work long hard hours, and a passion for their cause. They must be able to hop on a plane at a moment's notice, eat lunch at the country club with a donor's spouse, and present an honest appraisal of the organization's strengths and virtues. The best major gift people love their work; they can talk about money, negotiate with Wall Street financiers, and close a deal with grace.

Hire a Prospect Researcher

A strong researcher is the backbone of a prospect-centered major gifts operation. Culling information from appropriate sources about the interests, assets, and background of a potential donor often can mean the difference between a successful call and one that fails to develop a strong tie with the prospect. With time and access to professional training seminars, a prospect researcher can be trained on the job, but

Making a Long-term Investment

One school had a new "hot prospect" whose name surfaced through an alumni screening and rating program. The information eventually was passed on to the regional major gifts officer for that area. After several phone calls to line up an appointment, the staff member made a qualifying call to meet the prospect face to face.

She learned from her visit that the prospect had married a wealthy and philanthropic manufacturer, a philanthropist who supported his own alma mater with large gifts. At this point, the alumna was confirmed as a major gift prospect with a rating of $1 million.

The next step was to have the dean of the college meet with both the husband and wife. During that visit, the dean asked the couple to endow a faculty chair with a gift of $1 million. The couple agreed to consider that amount, but it took a second visit by the major gift officer and additional conversations with the dean to close the gift. The alumna was asked to join the college's board.

The couple went on to make additional gifts totaling more than $5 million to the college over a period of years. The initial process, from identification of the prospect to the first million-dollar gift, took 18 months, but the relationship developed into a lifetime of giving.

Major gifts take time to develop; consider them a long-term investment in the future of the institution.

a researcher hired with prior experience can add information to your program more quickly.

When hiring a professional researcher, look for a penchant for detail work, good organizational skills, and strong computer capabilities. Determination, focus, curiosity, and the patience to ferret out information and put it all together are important qualities for success in the research field. Finding a person of the highest level of integrity is also a key requirement. Often the researcher will work closely with volunteers, board members, and development staff to collect, process, and organize information about prospects.

Provide Administrative Support

Some major gift staff members (and volunteers) prefer to make their own appointments with prospects, especially those with whom they have developed strong relationships. For qualifying visits and most regular development travel, however, appointment setting can be a time-consuming and tricky proposition. Many potential donors are busy, elusive, and travel often from place to place.

A strong administrative staff member with good communications skills can pin down appointments, run lists, plan itineraries, coordinate travel plans, write introductory and thank-you letters, and generally keep the major gift staff and volunteers focused and supported on the home front. Coordinating the calendars of volunteers, executive directors, and board members for a call on a prospect can take hours.

A good development officer spends her time and energy out of the office, not behind the desk or on the computer. Although administrative staff can be shared with other advancement staff, it is inefficient to run a major gifts office without appropriate backup staff providing assistance for clerical and support duties.

Identify a Proposal Writer

Writing strong letters and proposals is a special skill that goes along with major gifts work. At some point in the cultivation and solicitation process, most prospective donors will require a proposal or written description of the proposed project. Many times the quality and content of the proposal is a key component of the decision to make a large gift, so the writer is an important member of the major gifts team. Often, proposals have to be tuned to the specific interest and background of the prospect, making them a creative challenge.

It can be difficult to identify, hire, and train skilled writers in nonprofit organizations. Asking for writing samples from qualified applicants is one way to find a

 RULES OF THE ROAD

It isn't an ask if you don't put a dollar amount on the table.

good staff member. Training or adding to the skill set of a person already on staff may be a good option; look for a publications person, public relations staff member, or highly qualified administrative assistant who knows the strong points of your organization and can express them well in writing.

If you don't wish to hire a full-time staff member, there are alternatives to consider to cover proposal writing and production. Some major gifts officers are good writers and prefer writing their own proposals. This allows them to match their prospects' interests closely, an important component of a prospect-centered approach to major gift work. Writing takes time, however, and can cause a major gift staff member to spend less time in face-to-face meetings with potential donors.

Another option is to hire a writer on a part-time basis to develop proposal and letter templates that can be edited and revised later for specific needs. Hiring one staff member to cover both research and writing responsibilities works for some advancement shops, although experience shows that the research component often suffers in this scenario. Whatever solution you choose, plan carefully to meet your writing needs as you build your major gifts program.

Staffing and Budget for a Major Gifts Program

Staffing and finding the resources to budget a major gift program require advance planning for organizations, whether they are small or large. Getting a major gifts program up and running can be a costly process. In the Midwest and southeastern sectors of the United States, major gifts officers are paid anywhere from $35,000 to $80,000, depending on the size of the organization and the experience of the candidate. On the East and West coasts, expect to pay $100,000 or more for an experienced major gift officer. Salaries usually are higher for those with campaign experience, for major gift directors, or for those in larger advancement shops.

Exhibit 2.1 illustrates the recommended staffing level for building a new program, based on hiring two major gifts officers and the additional team members needed to mount a successful program. If your organization can afford to hire only one major gifts professional, try to add at least one additional support staff member who can contribute some of the desired skills.

EXHIBIT 2.1

Recommended Staffing Level for a New Major Gifts Program

Position	# Staff
Major Gift Officers	2
Proposal Writer	1
Administrative/Appointment Secretary	1
Prospect Researcher	1
Total Staff Added	**5**

Add Travel Costs

You will also need to assess whether your organization will require a program that is local, regional, or national. This assessment will help you to estimate travel and program costs. It is much more expensive to run a national major gifts program than a local one, but your ability to access gifts from top prospects nationwide may end up paying for the extra costs of a broader, national program. Ultimately this decision should depend on where your prospects live. Estimated annual expenditures for travel will vary widely by organization and style of fundraising, but even in these days of electronic communication, some travel funding will be necessary to promote personal relationships with out-of-town prospects.

Assess Cultivation and Event Costs

Fundraising events, whether in your local area or in a number of cities where you have identified prospects, can add significantly to the cost of your advancement program if they are not reined in (see Exhibit 2.2). Event costs can be controlled by seeking out local hosts in each city, finding a setting that is contributed free of charge, and seeking local sponsors to help defray expenses. Often the personal relationships among staff, board members, and donors that form the core of a good major gift

EXHIBIT 2.2

Sample Annual Budget for a New Major Gifts Program

Salary and Benefits: Add 5 professionals*	$350,000
Travel: Visit 10 national cities 4 times/year	$ 80,000
Events: Hold 10 small group dinners	$ 50,000
Prospect Tracking System (add module)	$ 50,000
Prospect Research Tools	$ 25,000
Annual Base Budget	**$555,000**

*5 professional staff as identified in Exhibit 2.1.

program are not best served with large, grand events anyway. These relationships are best established through small group meetings in the prospect's home, intimate dinners hosted by supporters, and meals in private settings with several guests, which are all much less expensive than large fundraising gala events.

Hiring, Supervising, and Training for Success in Major Gifts

Finding and hiring experienced staff members can be a major challenge. The advancement field is attractive to a wide variety of people with relationship skills, but you will want to find the right match for your organization and your donors. Experience in asking for and closing gifts is important, especially if your program needs to produce results immediately. Watch out for job hoppers; some major gifts professionals spend their careers skipping from one nonprofit to another, pushing their salary levels up as they move on to each subsequent position.

It may be better in the long run for your institution to invest in an individual who already has the knowledge and commitment to your cause. Look at the advancement professionals already working for your organization. The annual fund

Where to Look for Major Gift Staff Members

- Select and train program directors or other senior staff from inside your organization.

- Promote an advancement staff member from within.

- Contact major gift officers in other local nonprofits.

- Attend local advancement professional group meetings to network.

- Look for board members or volunteers who have appropriate skills.

- Review lists of alumni and other prior users of your services.

- Ask your peers in other nonprofits for recommendations.

- Ask fundraising consultants for recommendations.

- Place ads locally, regionally, or nationally.

- Hire an executive search firm.

director, for instance, might be familiar with your constituencies and show promise for working with larger donors. Promoting from within can build loyalty and hold out the promise of career development for younger, less experienced staff.

Program directors, volunteers, or even board members who know your organization might fit in well if trained to make up for any specific skills they are lacking. Knowledge of the donor community can be a major benefit of hiring someone who is a known quantity. A candidate's organizational skills, passion for the cause, and willingness to ask often makes up for an initial lack of experience in dealing with major donors (see Exhibit 2.3).

Supervising Major Gift Officers

Structurally, the major gifts staff usually reports to either the major gifts director, who also takes on a group of prospects, or directly to the chief advancement officer. In some multidivisional organizations, such as universities, hospitals, or other

EXHIBIT 2.3

Skills and Characteristics of the Successful Major Gifts Officer

- Integrity of the highest standard

- Ability to work well with your executive director and board

- Strong oral and written communication skills

- Personal commitment to the mission and goals of your organization

- Good organizational and time management skills

- Knowledge of likely prospects

- Knowledge and prior use of prospect tracking information systems

- High level of energy and enthusiasm

- Willing to travel and work nights and weekends

- Ability to interact well with individuals in social and business settings

- Experience with donor cultivation and solicitation techniques

- Experience with gifts at the dollar level you desire for your program

- Exhibits flexibility and good humor under pressure

nonprofits with several independently budgeted units, each division has a major gift officer reporting separately to the director of each unit.

Although this type of "every unit on its own bottom" organizational structure can motivate strong performance and a positive competitive spirit, it can also get bogged down with duplicative administrative support networks, conflicting prospect clearance policies, and ugly nonproductive turf battles. A better approach is to build a central major gifts staff, then give them assignments to cover each unit in order to provide detailed knowledge of divisional needs and perspectives.

Supervising major gift staff members can be compared to running the sales staff of a large professional for-profit company. Staff members need to be carefully motivated, trained, compensated, and directed, but all with a light touch. If the

The Football Coach Factor

Why are major gifts officers able to command so much money? The argument goes that if one employee—say, the football coach—is responsible for bringing in a major percentage of the revenue and publicity for the organization, then that person deserves to be paid relative to his importance to the organization as a whole. In many universities today, the football coach is paid more than the president, and the university feels lucky to have attracted a winning coach at whatever the price.

Much the same story is true with major gift officers. If a trained, professional advancement staff member is paid $100,000 but brings in a gift of $5 million, the high salary is easy to justify.

TIPS & TECHNIQUES

AFP Code Regarding Compensation for Development Officers

The Association of Fundraising Professionals (AFP) has long regarded the payment of a percentage of the gift amount to development officers as an unethical practice. This is the actual language from the compensation section of the AFP Code of Ethical Principles and Standards of Professional Practice (amended 2004):

Members shall not accept compensation that is based on a percentage of contributions; nor shall they accept finder's fees.

Members may accept performance-based compensation, such as bonuses, provided such bonuses are in accord with prevailing practices within the members' own organizations, and are not based on a percentage of contributions.

Members shall not pay finder's fees, or commissions or percentage compensation based on contributions, and shall take care to discourage their organizations from making such payments.

supervisory role is too heavy-handed, then the entrepreneurial spirit will be beaten out of the group, leaving the organization with a team that spends more time making excuses than making appointments. But too little supervision can lead to cutting corners, conflicts of interest, and prospect calls that don't bring in anything toward the bottom line.

Most nonprofits do *not* pay major gift officers according to the amount of dollars they bring in. There are several reasons for this:

- The AFP considers paying a percentage of the gift, or paying finder's fees to the solicitor, to be unethical.

- Other advancement team members who contribute to a successful solicitation—such as researchers and writers—will not get the extra compensation.

- Volunteers and other staff, such as the president, who participate in a successful call do not get extra compensation.

- Donors do not want a portion of their gift going to any purpose other than the one for which the donation was directed.

- Many of the largest gifts are the result of long-term relationships developed over years between the donor and the nonprofit, and thus cannot be attributed to one staff member.

- A staff member might be motivated to close a smaller gift quickly, in order to contribute to his or her own compensation, and miss an opportunity to cultivate a donor toward a larger, lifetime gift.

If your organization wants to reward an advancement staff member for a job well done, consider setting up an annual bonus system for reaching certain established goals, financial and nonfinancial. Hiring at the going market rate and giving appropriate annual raises can help to attract and keep productive staff; this is probably not the place to try to hire the cheapest alternative. Perks that relate to the job might be attractive to productive staff members, ranging from a company car to country club memberships. Major gift professionals who travel heavily appreciate

TIPS & TECHNIQUES

How to Supervise Major Gift Staff Members

- Assign prospects by name to each major gift staff member.

- Assign regions or areas of responsibility to each major gift staff member.

- Set clear standards for what constitutes a contact with a prospect.

- Set quarterly goals for contacts with prospects.

- Develop a *moves management system* (see "What Is a Moves Management System?" section) to track and plan progress with prospects.

- Set annual goals for dollars raised.

- Set out clear provisions for conflict of interest.

- Meet monthly or quarterly with each staff member to review progress.

- Don't pay based on a percentage of the gifts brought in.

- Do consider giving a bonus if annual dollar goals are met or exceeded.

- Give credit where credit is due; most major gifts are a team effort.

being provided with laptops, cell phones with e-mail capability, and other accoutrements of modern life on the road. The bottom line is that your organization is investing heavily in building relationships between your donors and your staff, and you have to keep the staff in order to keep those relationships viable.

Troubleshooting with Major Gifts Staff

Organizations can have difficulty defining and integrating the role of major gift officer into their culture. Some expensive mistakes ensue. Here are some examples of real-world problems experienced when building a major gift staff.

- *Allow staff access to top prospects.* If a major gift staff member can't make calls on prospects who are wealthy, he can't raise big gifts.

- *Don't blindside the staff.* Communicate all contacts between the board, chief executive, and volunteers with prospects assigned to major gift staff.

- *Provide appropriate training and update regularly.* Major gift staff members must understand completely the programs and goals of the organization in order to represent them effectively with donors.

- *Don't hire someone because of family ties.* A major gift staff member is often the worst person to solicit family and friends, and hiring someone who can't be fired is never a good idea.

- *Don't allow discrimination in salaries, functions, or titles.* Often highly educated and assertive, major gift staff members are quick to note and take action against discriminatory policies, patterns, or treatment in an organization.

Training Major Gift Staff

There are two kinds of training issues with major gifts staff: gaining inside knowledge of the organization and learning the external skills—the fundraising techniques—needed to bring in larger gifts. Both areas require personalized training based on the staff member's background, experience, and needs.

Teaching about the organization itself may be easier for most nonprofits to provide, but often it is relegated to a subsidiary role or downplayed with new high-level professional staff. Consider designing a training program that can be utilized for new staff, volunteers, board members, and other potential insiders when needed.

Designing an in-house training program should involve some or all of these components:

- Tour of all facilities with knowledgeable staff

- Explanation of all major programs by program directors

- Exposure and conversation with program participants and graduates

- Financial training with the chief financial officer to include overview of budget, accounts, endowment, and fiscal issues

- Meeting with the chief executive officer and board chair to gain insight into vision, mission, and future plans

- Deep familiarity with all funding goals and needs, including capital projects, endowment, programs, and operational overhead

Advancement training in major gift solicitation is available now in many forms. Many professional organizations offer high-quality training at seminars all across the country for major gift staff, chief executives, volunteers, deans, and other professionals who need to learn how to ask for money. Look up the national programs and conferences offered by AFP, the Council for Advancement and Support of Education (CASE), and the American Association of Museums (AAM). Also watch for workshops in your own community sponsored by the United Way, which offers training for organizations that receive funding through their programs, and others.

Effective training can also be provided on site through tapes, seminars, and consultants hired to provide personal time with your new staff. Role playing is a useful method for working with new major gift officers, because various scenarios can be played out by staff and volunteers. It is also useful for major gift staff members to have a familiarity with the basics of planned giving, which can be taught by an expert on staff or a consultant brought in for that purpose.

An informal but effective way to learn about major gift fundraising is to shadow an experienced professional or volunteer. Identify someone you know who is experienced with personal solicitations, perhaps someone already connected to your organization as a volunteer, board member, or donor. Ask that person to sit down with your new staff members to discuss their technique, then plan some calls together to visit prospects. Discuss the calls both before and after to gain insights into roles, handling objections, and closing the gift. Pairing new staff with experienced fundraisers is a wonderful way to share information, learn from each other, and build a strong cadre of solicitors. No matter how many seminars you attend or books you read, there is no substitute for learning from face-to-face experiences with real donors in real-life situations.

Pray for Understanding

The new building for the homeless shelter was being dedicated. The ceremony was scheduled to recognize the big naming gift, which had been made by a donor from a prominent Jewish family. The nonprofit, in keeping with the donor's traditions, had invited the local rabbi to deliver the invocation at the ceremony. All went smoothly until the chairman of the shelter's board, a devout Baptist, stood up to speak.

"We thank God for the Christian charity that went into the support for this building," intoned the man. A convulsive shudder ran like a wave through the attending crowd.

Prospect Tracking and Management Systems

Most development information systems providers now offer prospect management and tracking modules as part of their ongoing systems support. Adding a prospect tracking module probably will raise the cost of your information systems and increase system use by staff, and might require new or updated PC support. Many major gift officers now travel with laptops and connect to the home system through the Internet from the road to download information, update files, and gain access to research and giving reports. You will need to talk with your systems provider to understand the options available to you and the additional costs for both software and equipment.

It is possible to run a prospect tracking system for a small major gifts effort on Excel, Access, or other proprietary database operations. Although this is more effective than the old method of keeping a file box on hand with index cards for each prospect, the goal is to have an efficient and accessible means of keeping and sharing information about specific prospects by name. Once your organization decides to hire several major gift staff members, raise more than a couple of million dollars, or has more than a few hundred prospects to track, it is wise to invest in a more flexible system that will meet your needs across the board.

What Is a Moves Management System?

At its most basic level, a moves management system is a method for planning and tracking each contact, known as a move, that either has been taken or is planned to be taken with a prospect. Usually this tracking is now done through a computerized database, although hand-tracking systems may be more comfortable for technophobes. When a development officer is responsible for the cultivation and solicitation of a hundred or more individuals, systematic planning and tracking of contacts becomes important.

Of course, systems are useful only when they are used; requiring major gift staff to enter prospect contacts into the prospect tracking system is usually an important ground rule. Consider setting a policy that if no computer record of a contact exists, it means that no contact was made. If the staff is then evaluated by the number of contacts made, the problem will resolve itself.

These entries may be made by the major gift officer for each of his prospects, or entries can be passed on to a data clerk or secretary if one is available (see Exhibit 2.4). The supervisor should have access to the entire database for review on a regular basis, with standard reports showing the number of calls made and by whom, the dollars asked for, and future contacts planned. Special reports pulling prospects by region, interest area, and dollar level are also useful. If future moves planned are always entered with a proposed action date, the tracking system can become a powerful tool that produces weekly or monthly reminders for pending activity.

Ideally, the moves management system, if used properly, also can become an important tool for projecting the dollar value of solicitations, gifts, and project support for the entire advancement organization. As such, it becomes a financial planning tool as well as a prospect management tool. The system also can be linked to an events management module; if, for instance, the next "move" or planned contact for a prospect is to be invited to your annual fundraising black tie dinner, entering this move can prompt an invitation to be flagged for the event director.

Identifying Major Gift Prospects

Now that you have your staff hired, trained, and ready to go, who are they going to call on? Prospect identification and research is one of the fastest-growing areas in

EXHIBIT 2.4

Sample Entries in a Moves Management System

- Prospect's name

- Prospect's contact information: telephone, fax, e-mail

- Prospect's home and business address, city, state, and zip

- Prospect's area of interest within the organization (i.e., "endowment")

- Name of staff person assigned to the prospect (prospect manager)

- Ask level: dollar level or rating for a solicitation

- Expected gift level: dollar level or rating for anticipated gift

- Readiness level: how close the prospect is to making a gift

- Last contact: contact type, date, and outcome

- Next contact: proposed next contact type and date

- Future contacts: with proposed dates

- Link to stewardship plan

- Link to research profile

- Link to donor's past giving record

the advancement enterprise. The better that your organization can strategically pinpoint who your best prospects are likely to be, the more efficiently and cost-effectively you can build relationships, develop your prospects' giving potential, and encourage them to invest in your organization.

Not all the names on your initial list will be prospects capable of making a gift of $10,000 or $100,000, not to mention $1 million. Many will not have the means to contribute a gift of this size. Some will not be interested enough in your organization to make a contribution. There will probably be more names on the list than your major gifts staff can hope to visit with and get to know personally. How do you begin to sort out the real prospects from those who are just names on a list?

First You Make a List

Your first job is to create a databank of potential supporters. Some sources for prospect names are listed in Exhibit 2.5. Begin by reviewing the names of all those who touch your organization in any meaningful way. It is less useful just to store up the names of wealthy people in your community, although reviewing such names with your board on a regular basis is not a bad idea. Generally, the presence of a connection to your cause, if not specifically to your organization, is required to turn an individual from a "suspect" into a "prospect."

Note that several of the sources listed require other members of the organization to share information with the advancement team. Collecting the names of volunteers, visitors, and Web site hits may require teamwork across departmental lines, which can be daunting in some organizations. It is useful to educate everyone in the organization about the importance of identifying major donors, because receptionists, tour guides, and program directors are most likely to be on the front lines when a big potential prospect calls or appears. Make sure the lines of communication are open, and give credit publicly to those who support your efforts.

Identify one or more people who will be responsible for prospect identification, qualification, and research efforts. If there is a professional researcher on staff, this person is the best choice; other possibilities include the donor database manager, a major gifts officer, an executive assistant, or the development director.

Conceptually, the goal is to move prospect names through a process from a broad list of names initially identified as *suspects* through several cuts to reach a smaller list of *major gift prospects* who have been qualified through personal face-to-face meetings (see Exhibit 2.6). With the appropriate tools and staff in place, this process can allow an organization to develop a real base of major gift prospects in six months to a year from the initiation of the prospect identification program.

Electronic Prospect Screening

Electronic prospect screening has become a popular method for making a first cut into an organization's prospect list in our age of widely available online information. Many

EXHIBIT 2.5

Sources of Potential Prospect Names

- Past and current donors to your organization.

- Members of your organization.

- Past users of your services (i.e., alumni, grateful patients, etc.).

- Individuals who made gifts to other organizations with a mission similar to yours.

- Parents and family members of those who used your services.

- Corporations that market to audiences similar to those you serve.

- Foundations that give in your area of focus (i.e., education, arts).

- Wealthy individuals in your community.

- Family foundations in your region.

- Review lists with your volunteers and board members.

- Collect names and addresses of all visitors and volunteers.

- Capture names of visitors to your Web site.

- Buy selected lists from a reputable list broker.

- Swap lists with related organizations.

- Keep the annual donor lists of peer organizations.

- Reach out to local experts in estate planning, including bank trust officers, lawyers, and accountants.

- Review lists of your vendors annually.

- Read the business news in your region.

EXHIBIT 2.6

Top Prospect Identification

1. Identify a broad list of names drawn from all sources (see Exhibit 2.5).

2. Hire an electronic screening firm to screen the entire list.

3. Conduct a screening and rating program to review the entire list.

4. Analyze results and review top prospects with staff, board members, and experienced volunteers.

5. Prioritize top prospects for personal qualifying meetings with advancement staff.

6. Conduct individual research on top prospects who have been qualified through the process above.

---

for-profit firms now offer electronic methods of screening large numbers of prospect names in a database for a fee, often based on the number of names screened. These firms usually rely on publicly available data, although there are some proprietary lists and databases that distinguish one firm from another.

Before signing on with one of these firms, ask the representative to run a test, using names in your own database run through their screening program. Also make sure that the data output is in a format that is useful to you. Determine in advance if the data you will receive can be loaded or added to the development information system you are currently running, with ties to the prospect's record, to allow easy access by your researchers and major gift officers.

Most electronic prospect research companies offer access to information culled from a variety of sources (see Exhibit 2.7). These sources are also available to your research staff, although some have a hefty fee attached, and you may want to invest in one or more of them for ongoing research capabilities. The advantage of the screening firm, however, is that it can take your entire database and run it against several databases concurrently, spitting out a list of "hits" for your staff to follow up on. Thus an electronic prospect screening service provides more information, on a much faster basis, than you could provide working on your own.

EXHIBIT 2.7

Common Sources of Data for Electronic Prospect Screening Programs

- **Standard and Poor's** (information on publicly held companies)

- **Dun & Bradstreet** (includes data on private companies)

- Real estate holdings (often provided by **Lexis Nexis**)

- **Lexis Nexis Development Universe** (online search capability that provides access to newspaper articles and other public information, searchable by name)

- Foundation guide (i.e., **Guidestar** or the **Foundation Directory**)

- **SEC data** on insider stock trading (used for researching corporate officers and large stockholders in public companies)

- **Marquis Who's Who** listings (provides personal biographical data)

In essence, electronic screening is a quick summary of the research process that highlights names you will want to have your staff review for a next cut. It is not a substitute for intensive research on prospects whom your organization does not know well. Electronic prospect screening will not tell you about a prospect's passion for your cause; it will not tell you whether he is a private investor in mutual funds, or whether she is starting a new business.

Books like *The Millionaire Next Door* have shown us that much wealth in the United States is hidden and cannot be identified through publicly available sources. Even with its recognized limitations, however, electronic screening is a useful tool that can provide a good snapshot to help determine which prospects should get moved to the next tier of prospect identification and research.

Screening and Rating Sessions

Prospect screening and rating is a common technique used to help prioritize and rate lists of prospects. Usually screening sessions are held with small groups of volunteers or institutional supporters who are invited to a special session for the purpose of prospect review. These groups meet to review lists of prospect names and use their personal knowledge of the individuals being screened to identify prospects who might be able to make gifts at certain prespecified levels. Screening can be done either silently, with each member of the group working on her own individualized list, or out loud, with all members of the group contributing to a discussion about each name on the list. Often, members of the group are already donors to the organization and are asked to participate in this type of session on a confidential basis.

Screening also can be done with groups that already exist to assist the nonprofit, such as boards and advisory groups. Making prospect screening session the focus of a board meeting can help draw attention to a new major gifts program or to a pending campaign. Sometimes board members or volunteers are reluctant to speak about the personal wealth of their friends, especially in front of a large group. If you sense a reluctance to share information, ask to meet privately with your volunteer to secure appropriate information in a confidential setting.

Many development officers also screen lists one-on-one routinely as an element of their personal calls on major gift prospects. Most wealthy donors will know or be able to identify peers in their community who might also have an interest in the organization. Asking a potential donor to assist with the identification of other prospects is also a practical way to create a tie between a prospect and the organization's funding initiatives.

Screening and rating of prospects should be an ongoing process. Although there may be an intense focus on these methods at the beginning of a campaign or a major gifts effort, it should be incorporated as a systematic element in the advancement plan. University alumni reunions, for instance, often include an opportunity to update and share information on potential donors who might be known only to peers in that class. The purpose of screening and rating on a regular basis is to update information and bring attention to those who have recently acquired wealth.

Making Qualifying Calls

The purpose of screening and rating programs is to winnow the prospect list down to a manageable number of potential names and to prioritize those names. Once that

How to Conduct a Prospect Screening and Rating Session

1. Identify and meet with a volunteer screening chair. Discuss what you will do and how you will do it so there are no surprises.

2. Identify a small group to invite to the session; consider hosting sessions in key cities, for instance.

3. Prepare a letter over the volunteer's signature to invite the selected group to the screening session.

4. Host the session in a private place, such as a conference room or a hotel meeting room.

5. Use electronic screening results to prioritize names for review, if your organization has done such screening.

6. Arrange prospect lists by business, geographic area, or by age (i.e., class year) so that screeners can match their own profile.

7. Provide an introduction to the session to explain what you are doing and why. Ask the host to speak briefly.

8. Assure the screeners of complete confidentiality.

9. Do screening either silently, with each member of the group working on their own list, or out loud, with all members of the group reviewing the same list.

10. Ask your screeners to check boxes to indicate responses to these questions:

    - How much could the prospect give if motivated?

    - Do they know something about the prospect that they are willing to share with you?

    - Are they willing to introduce someone in the organization to the prospect?

11. Thank them and follow up privately with those who agree to open the door with prospects.

12. Set up a system to organize, process, and enter the information into the database back at the office.

goal has been reached, personal qualifying calls can begin. Most major gift officers spend a majority of their time meeting people and talking with them in an attempt to determine if they are truly good prospects or not. This time, usually spent in a face-to-face meeting, is known as the qualifying call (see Exhibit 2.8).

The purpose of the qualifying call is to determine if the prospect meets certain criteria for being considered a major gift prospect for your organization. These criteria can be set in a flexible manner, but the list usually includes:

- An assessment or rating of giving capacity

- The level of interest shown in the organization's mission and goals

- Willingness to become involved in the work of the organization

- An assessment of the willingness to make a gift

Although it can be a controversial first step, many experienced development officers like to ask for a small gift on the first call with a prospect in order to assess the individual's philanthropic intent, level of interest, and willingness to provide support for the nonprofit.

Advancement professionals call this a "cultivation gift" and consider it a first step in the longer process of cultivating the prospect for a larger gift as the relationship with the prospect reaches maturity. Asking for a small annual gift or soliciting a membership-level contribution can also be a good way to add the prospect to the mailing list, which keeps the prospect updated on the activities, news, and progress of the organization.

A Note on Confidentiality

Recently, several nonprofits that promised confidentiality to donors have come under fire for using prospect research services. It can be unnerving to donors to know that the dollar value of their stock holdings in publicly held companies, the real estate value of their primary and vacation homes, their published biographical data, and their family foundation giving records have all been distributed to a volunteer for the purpose of soliciting them for a gift. Even though all of these records are publicly available, and the use of such information is considered to be both legal

EXHIBIT 2.8

Elements of the Qualifying Call

1. Wealth Assessment: Is the prospect capable of making a major gift?

- Identify cues to wealth, such as home value, second homes, cars, jewelry, trips made, business information shared, etc.

- Look for expensive personal interests, such as art collecting, Alpine skiing, horse breeding, mountain climbing, etc.

2. Philanthropic Assessment: Is the prospect likely to make a major gift?

- Ask the prospect what other nonprofits he supports.

- Ask what other boards or organizations he volunteers for.

- Ask him to prioritize his philanthropic interests and see where your organization stands.

3. Level of Interest: Is the prospect interested in the mission and goals of the organization?

- Introduce organizational information through discussion, brochures, or videos.

- Ask the prospect for his reaction, listen, and respond with care.

4. Involvement: Is the prospect willing to become more involved with the organization, and if so, in what way?

- Prepare options for involvement to offer, such as hosting an event in his home, volunteering with a program, or agreeing to visit the organization's site.

- Ask if he will meet with you or another member of your organization again to continue building the relationship.

5. Giving: Is the prospect willing to make a gift to the organization?

- Many experienced major officers ask for a small gift on their first visit with a prospect. Willingness to buy a membership or make a small annual gift indicates buy-in and paves the way for future support and ties with the organization.

and ethical, relationships with donors in the nonprofit world can be extremely sensitive and must be treated with caution.

It is the responsibility of the advancement team to see that personal information about donors is used and distributed appropriately. In many shops, access to research data is limited to staff only, with ratings and profiles cleared of confidential information for use by outside volunteers and board members. Other organizations agree to provide personal wealth information to fundraising volunteers, but limit the review of research profiles to in-house meetings and collect the materials afterward. It is a good idea to mark all research profiles and ratings with a **CONFIDENTIAL** stamp and think twice before copying, distributing, e-mailing, or faxing confidential information to anyone. Use of a good shredder is also recommended.

Summary

Building a major gifts program requires hiring staff, developing and finding resources for a budget, and providing program support within the advancement operation. Major gift officers need support from a team of advancement specialists, which include researchers, writers, and administrative assistants. The data information system used in the advancement operation may need to be augmented with a prospect management tracking module. Staff members will need to be hired, trained, and supervised by someone with the expertise and management skills to keep them motivated and productive.

A major gifts program also requires a concerted effort to build a prospect base of potential major gift donors. This can be accomplished with the help of a staff researcher, an electronic prospect screening program, and qualification calls by major gift staff members. Developing an ongoing program for screening and rating prospects with a cadre of knowledgeable supporters is also a prerequisite for prospect identification and rating over the long term. All of the information collected on a prospect should be treated confidentially and managed by professionally trained staff members.

CHAPTER 3

Board Leadership

After reading this chapter you will be able to:

- Develop and train board leaders
- Promote board leadership in fundraising
- Integrate efforts of board and staff to raise more dollars

Developing Board Leadership

Experienced advancement professionals will attest to the fact that strong board leadership is an essential component of a successful fundraising program. But what does board leadership really mean, and how is the role of the nonprofit board changing? Nonprofits today need to have a proactive plan to build their boards and train their leaders to take on key roles, from fundraising to financial oversight.

The Changing Nature of Nonprofit Board Leadership

A spate of recent business scandals in the for-profit world, from Enron to WorldCom, has focused attention on the responsibilities of corporate board members. With the advent of Sarbanes-Oxley, the 2002 corporate reform law now in place, corporate board members have to be much more attuned to the financial and governance practices of the company they serve as directors. Corporate directors are now being required to take on more responsibility for issues that once were considered the sole domain of the president and chief executive officer, such as executive compensation, accounting practices, competitive business strategies, and high-risk investments. Legally, ethically, and financially, the role of being a corporate director has changed to focus on responsibility and accountability.

This same emphasis on transparency and credibility has now reached the nonprofit world. Many nonprofits have adopted the governance practices of Sarbanes-Oxley, even though the law doesn't apply to them. Some nonprofit trustees, familiar with the new corporate demands for accountability, are demanding more financial controls in order to enhance the credibility of the nonprofits they work with. Other trustees, worried that sloppy governance will tarnish their own reputations, are reviewing audits and fiscal policies with an eye toward staving off claims of financial mismanagement.

The regulatory climate also has changed dramatically for nonprofits over the past few years. The United States Congressional Senate Finance Committee has been leading the charge by putting charitable organizations, including private foundations, under intense scrutiny (see Exhibit 3.1). A slew of nonprofits, from the Red Cross to the United Way, has been the subject of investigations that have reviewed management practices, governance structures, fundraising tactics, and financial reporting.

The government's stated goal is to close tax loopholes, clamp down on fraud and tax abuse, press for the disclosure of more information to the public, and improve the oversight of charitable programs. These are worthy goals. In meeting these goals, however, some institutions feel that the investigative process has been heavy-handed, casting a shadow on nonprofits that are operating legally and ethically. Others in the nonprofit world have welcomed the attention, claiming that increased accountability will only add to the credibility of the sector, building additional trust and communication among donors, boards, and nonprofits.

Whatever their opinion of the government's role, nonprofit executives have found that the changing climate is thrusting boards into playing a more demanding and active role. Board members are now becoming involved in the oversight of

---

EXHIBIT 3.1

Nonprofit Practices Currently under Review by Federal Investigators

- Financial agreements between charities and insurance companies

- Charitable tax shelters

- Fraudulent solicitation appeals

- Valuation practices for noncash donations, including land and automobiles

- The role of tax-exempt institutions in the financing of global terrorism

- The tax-exempt status of certain types of nonprofits

- "Excessive" compensation and other perks for nonprofit executives

---

charitable giving policies, including the valuation of noncash gifts, ventures with for-profit companies, and meeting new financial reporting standards. Board members are also taking the lead in financial accounting to assure donors that contributions are well used and well invested, and that the organization is doing what it said it would do with their contributions.

Transparency and accountability have become institutional goals for nonprofits and their boards.

Building Your Board

In order to build a board that can take ownership and provide an appropriate degree of oversight and leadership, it is useful to step back and analyze the board's membership and degree of involvement in the organization. This assessment process can be informal, using a list of questions similar to those that follow, or it can take a more formal turn by bringing in an outside consultant to study the board and make recommendations on appropriate changes. Sometimes it is useful to make a board assessment part of a broader strategic planning effort across the organization.

TIPS & TECHNIQUES

Assessing the Board's Leadership Quotient

- Does the board have representation from all the different parts of the community that the nonprofit serves? (Plan for diversity of ethnic background, age, sex, and religion.)

- Does the board have the appropriate geographic representation to represent the nonprofit's outreach efforts?

- Does the board have representation from a variety of business sectors that are important in the community, such as banking, real estate, energy, manufacturing, agriculture, finance, and the like?

- Does the board have review and oversight of fundraising policies, including gift valuation, gift accounting, direct mail solicitation, staff compensation, and planned giving programs?

- Does the board have members who are familiar with nonprofit accounting and governance practices?

- Does the board have access to audits, budgets, and other information related to the organization's financial practices?

- Has the organization identified and prepared the next generation of leaders for the board?

- Is there a clear understanding of the board's overall role and fundraising expectations when new members are invited onto the board?

- Is there an in-depth orientation program for new board members?

- Are board members knowledgeable and passionate about the work of the organization?

If your board comes up weak on several points, think about making changes in the board structure, membership, or recruitment procedures before you begin your new major gifts program. You might want to revamp the nominating process, set up a new process for training future leaders, or expand the board to include more national members. Although it is important to have board members who bring a wide variety of skills, it is also important to have some members who can give large gifts and some who can ask for large gifts—and they aren't always the same people!

Many new board members complain that they are never told exactly what the expectations are for their involvement before they agree to join a nonprofit board. This area is rife for misunderstanding, especially when financial contributions are part of the equation. Think carefully about the expectations you have of your board and how you communicate these expectations to new board members. Some boards write out a set of board responsibilities and use these when recruiting new members.

Training Your Board

No board member will arrive with all the information and skills needed to serve your organization well. Consider setting up an in-house orientation program to provide new board members with information that is specific to your organizational needs (see Exhibit 3.2). Then follow up with annual updates for current board members to keep everyone posted on program and governance changes. Keep the updates light and fun for everyone by opening with a quick organizational trivia quiz, or do a scavenger hunt that introduces board members to areas of the nonprofit's program they haven't yet encountered.

Training also can be provided for specific needs, such as accounting or fundraising. Finance committee members, for instance, must be able to read financial reports and budgets as well as understand the financial reporting requirements for nonprofits. An organization's auditors might be hired to run a training session for audit and finance committee members, or a savvy board member can help to bring new committee members up to speed on financial issues. Outside investment advisors also are helpful in running sessions for board committees on the financial side of the organization.

Many nonprofits provide fundraising training sessions on-site for development committee members. Consider, also, that in advance of a new major gift outreach effort, it may be appropriate to provide training for the entire board. In-house advancement staff can be used to provide training, but an outside consultant sometimes

TIPS & TECHNIQUES

Discussion Points When Recruiting New Board Members

1. Communicate the expected level of giving by board members to the organization.

2. Identify specific areas in which all board members must partici-pate, such as fundraising, program development, or community outreach.

3. If mounting a new fundraising effort, outline expectations.

4. Discuss the time commitment that will be expected:

   a. Number of annual meetings

   b. Number of committees they will be asked to join and choices for committee assignments

   c. Committee meeting frequency and responsibilities

   d. Annual events they may be expected to attend

5. Clarify the length of the term that will be served and any term limits to membership.

6. Review conflict-of-interest policy and discuss any areas of potential difficulty.

7. Discuss the board orientation process and expectations about how the new member will become familiar with the organization.

grabs the attention of board members more effectively. The trainer can provide ideas for effective cultivation activities, act out solicitation techniques, explain planned giving vehicles, and demonstrate how to close an ask. Using video, PowerPoint, and other interactive teaching techniques is helpful to keep board members focused and engaged; just as in the classroom, most board members don't like being talked at. Role-playing is always an effective teaching tool in fundraising.

EXHIBIT 3.2

Sample Orientation Program for New Board Members

8:00 A.M.	Continental breakfast and welcome by chairman of the board.
8:30 A.M.	Tour of the facility; include 5-minute overview by program directors of major programs.
9:30 A.M.	Meet with selected current and former beneficiaries of the nonprofit's services in an informal, roundtable format.
10:30 A.M.	Director of advancement makes presentation on fundraising plans, issues, and expectations. Take questions.
11:00 A.M.	CEO and finance director make presentation on accounting, governance, and long-term goals of the organization. Take questions.
Noon	Serve lunch; mix in small groups with board and staff; promote informal communication and exchanges.

Other methods of training board members in fundraising techniques (besides holding training sessions on-site) may be even more effective in the long run (see Tips & Techniques, "Training Techniques for Board Members and Volunteers"). Find ways to get board members face to face with real prospects and real donors to your organization so that they will understand intuitively the motivation, drive, and techniques that move donors to contribute to your cause. These techniques will also work with other volunteers who will be fundraising for your organization.

Board Leadership in Fundraising

Leadership in Fundraising: Give or Get

The old adage for board members, "Give or get," still holds true for most nonprofits. The bottom line is that, although increasing responsibilities are being placed on the shoulders of nonprofit board members, charitable giving remains the most

TIPS & TECHNIQUES

Training Techniques for Board Members and Volunteers

- Have volunteers participate in off-site workshops and seminars sponsored by professional fundraising associations.

- Bring a consultant on-site to provide personalized training sessions.

- Have an advancement staff member work one-on-one with board members and accompany them on calls with major gift prospects.

- Have experienced board members work one-on-one with new board members and accompany them on calls with major gift prospects.

- Have volunteers learn how to make smaller solicitations first, by participating in phonathons or annual giving programs.

- Arrange a focus group of current donors to your organization and invite board members to be the audience. Ask the donors to discuss what motivated them to give to your organization.

- Develop a survey instrument for current donors, asking them why they gave to your organization. Give each volunteer the names of three donors; have them conduct an interview, using the survey instrument.

important way that a board can show leadership and set the pace for moving the organization forward.

Giving generously, from both the heart and the bank account, is the *sine qua non* of board participation. Giving to one's potential is the bar by which a board member should be judged. Most observers, especially peers, will take note if the board member's gift falls into the token category. Of course, one man's token gift is another's lifetime contribution, and personal financial capabilities and circumstances enter heavily into the equation. As noted, it is also incumbent on the organization to make sure that new board members are told what the expectations are for giving during the board recruitment process.

Training Resistance

Some board members will resist training, and some will stick to bad habits acquired over years of volunteer work. What to do?

One nonprofit had a prominent donor and board member, a co-chair of the fundraising drive, who just couldn't get to the ask. He talked passionately about the cause (a new building) and was eager to meet with all the top prospects, but no one at the nonprofit could be sure that a dollar amount would ever be brought up in the conversation. He would make calls on prospects, report that they intended to "do something" for the building, but no gift would ever materialize.

Frustrated, the nonprofit's executive director wanted to stop using the co-chair on calls. The advancement director came up with a better idea: She proposed accompanying their difficult co-chair on calls to help move the conversation in the right direction. The team worked beautifully; the co-chair displayed his passion in making the case for the gift, then the advancement director made a request for a specific dollar amount of funding. Gifts began to be pledged, and the co-chair was able to bask in the results of his successful fundraising.

It is the board that "sets the pace" during any major gift fundraising drive, both by giving early and by giving to capacity. It is almost magical to note how a "stretch" gift from a committed board member can inspire others, both on the board and in the broader community. Many prospects, when asked for a major gift, will inquire what the nonprofit board has given; some will base their gift size on the response. Because of the enormous impact that board giving can have on the size of gifts received from others during a drive for major gifts, gifts from the board must be asked for early in a drive and carefully planned to create the maximum strategic effect.

Most organizations find that board solicitations are best conducted by board members, peer to peer. Often the executive director or the chief advancement officer will also be involved in these early calls. Sometimes the chair of the board will be asked first, as a way of recognizing her leadership, or a small group of committed board members, such as the executive committee, is approached first. Whatever the

The Farsighted Volunteer

The chair of the campaign, an old hand at fundraising, was making a call on the brash young real estate developer. He was given a written briefing on the call from the development office, which set the ask at $100,000.

After a pleasant discussion, the chair popped the question on the developer: "Would you be willing to support us with a gift of $1 million?" The developer took a deep breath and replied: "That sounds like a lot for me, but I could do $500,000."

"What happened in there? I thought we were going to ask for $100,000," the delighted director asked her chair after the call. "Oh, I forgot my glasses," said the man. "I couldn't read your briefing, so I just asked for what I thought we needed."

order, it is important to approach several members at the outset who can make gifts that are large enough to set a compelling example for others who follow.

Whether it is due to peer influence, a shared assessment of need, or a kind of group mentality, major gifts from board members often tend to cluster around a particular dollar level in a fundraising effort. Often board members at the same organization tend to share a similar business or social milieu, which encourages a competitive giving response. In any case, it tends to be true that if an organization secures three to four early gifts of $1 million from board members, the gifts that follow will cluster around the $1 million level. However, if the same group, with the same financial capability, finds that early gifts have clustered around $10,000, then the donors who follow will give only $10,000. This experience with gift clusters implies that fundraisers should try to close early gifts at as high a level as possible to set a high bar for early gifts from peers when starting their solicitation activity.

Board members, whether they give a lot or a little, can also be extremely effective at asking others to give. Many times a board member can open doors to prospects for whom the nonprofit's staff cannot gain access. In other situations, a board member may be able to motivate a prospect by explaining why he made his own gift. Finally, if the board member is willing to disclose the amount of her gift, she can influence the level of a prospective donor's contribution by suggesting a match or equivalent donation.

Beyond Give or Get

What about organizations where the board members don't have the means to make large gifts or access to those who do? Sometimes nonprofits seem to follow the old rule that "the rich get richer"—that is, groups with wealthy board members, who make big gifts, use their connections to solicit their wealthy friends, who make more big gifts, thus expanding the arena of haves and have-nots into the nonprofit sector.

Some boards just aren't comprised of people who have the means to make five-, six-, and seven-figure gifts. Many community-based nonprofits, for instance, draw their board members from lower-income groups who not only can't give, but they don't have the access to those who can. There are many options for boards to pursue in moving to strengthen their ability to give or get major gifts (see Exhibit 3.3).

Don't assume that your board members can't help you raise big gifts just because they aren't wealthy or important in the community pecking order. Ask your board members to accompany other volunteers, staff, or consultants on calls to underline the passion and commitment they have for your cause. There are many additional ways that a board member or other willing volunteer can help an organization to raise major gifts beyond *give or get*.

A creative advancement director or executive director will find that there are other ways to tap into the energy, enthusiasm, knowledge, commitment, and time of those who are ready to help. The donation of professional services, for instance, can allow a willing volunteer to provide high-quality legal, financial, or public relations (PR) support for the organization as it reaches out to new constituencies.

EXHIBIT 3.3

Ways to Strengthen Organizational Capacity for Raising Major Gifts

- Reconstitute the board membership by enlarging it or adding national representatives.

- Identify and recruit new members who bring access to wealth and/or major gift fundraising experience.

- Provide fundraising training for your board with a workshop given by an experienced professional.

- Create a separate volunteer committee focused on major gifts fundraising, drawn from the ranks of supporters who can make larger gifts.

- Hire a CEO and advancement staff members who have the appropriate skills and connections within the prospect community.

- Hire a fundraising consultant who has a successful track record with the prospects that you will be approaching.

Techniques for Sight-Raising with Your Board and Key Volunteers

Sometimes nonprofit volunteers and leaders who are well-meaning, devoted supporters of the nonprofit don't quite understand what it will take to meet the financial goals of the organization. They may make major gifts, but not quite as generously as you think they could; or they may be hesitant to make a commitment to a major gift, preferring to make smaller annual gifts to operations. A longtime board member might say, "I'll wait to see how many new donors respond before I make my gift," or she might make a token gift, waiting to see what others will do.

Through a series of techniques known as "sight-raising," you can work with and influence the gift levels of your key volunteers and board members who will be setting the pace for others throughout your fundraising drive (see "Tips & Techniques"). Sight-raising is really a form of strategic marketing, but it is marketing the needs and goals of your institution to your inner circle of supporters.

TIPS & TECHNIQUES

The Role of Board Members in a Major Gifts Program

- Reviewing lists of prospects to identify and rate potential major donors

- Introducing staff members to potential donors

- Hosting a small event for major prospects in home or office

- Appearing in a video or supplying a quote for materials

- Donating professional expertise, such as PR, legal services, design work

- Becoming an informed advocate, helping to "spread the word"

- Going along on calls to help "make the case" with a prospective donor

- Attending a training session to learn how to solicit and close a major gift

- Assisting in hiring and orienting new major gift staff members

- Reviewing policies and procedures for gift solicitation and accounting

- Participating in a strategic planning effort to determine how new funds will be used to meet the nonprofit's mission and goals

- Helping to develop investment policies for gifts

- Asking for major gifts

- Giving a major gift!

Although the techniques for sight-raising involve presenting and soliciting higher gift levels from the board and key volunteer leaders, they also provide community-wide recognition for donors who have committed to early major gifts. It is important to recognize that early leadership gifts ultimately will make a difference in the successful completion of a project or drive. Early PR and recognition for larger gifts is a key component to building momentum for a major gift fundraising effort. Whether this publicity comes from your own newsletter, a report to your

Sight-Raising Methods with Your Board

1. Make sure that your board thoroughly understands and supports the need for the project at hand.

2. Keep the board interested and involved with architectural drawings, project updates, financial reports, tours of the project, and funding reports.

3. Set an internal leadership level for individual gifts as a focus point for your work with board members.

4. Present the board with a list of naming opportunities and prices for the project, and set the highest options at leadership levels.

5. Announce early leadership gifts to the full board in order to build interest and momentum in the drive.

6. Develop a recognition plan for early large gifts, for instance, by profiling donors at this level in your newsletter.

7. Develop a visible method for recognizing board gifts at the leadership level, such as in an annual report.

8. Solicit early board gifts at the leadership level, and ask these donors to help you solicit the remaining board members.

board, or a profile in *The Wall Street Journal's* weekly column on philanthropy depends on whom you want to reach and how good your PR director is!

Using Challenges to Raise Bigger Gifts

Another effective method for raising the sights of prospects and donors capable of giving larger gifts is setting up a challenge. Most fundraisers are familiar with small gift challenges, which often come at the end of a campaign or annual fund drive, and seek to bring in lots and lots of little gifts. Challenges also can appeal to the competitive spirits of those who make larger gifts.

The structure of a challenge is limited only by your imagination. Challenges can set specific dollar goals, participation goals, or both; they can challenge gifts from individuals or groups; they can have a specific timetable or be completely open-ended. Some boards will set a dollar goal for all board gifts, kicked off by a challenge from a small group of top donors. A challenge can take the form of requesting second gifts from board members who have already given once to a project that needs an additional infusion.

In practice, although most donors will make good on their challenge gift even if the terms are not met, it is not wise to accept a challenge if you truly doubt your organization's ability to meet the terms. Some donors are not very susceptible to responding to what other donors give and find challenges annoying. Others, especially those who display entrepreneurial behavior in their own business practices, enjoy the one-upsmanship implied by creating or matching another's largesse.

IN THE REAL WORLD

A Challenge That Missed Its Goal

Sometimes challenges can be, well, *too challenging*. In one museum, a campaign was put together to raise $10 million for a new educational facility. A known number of wealthy major donors had been affiliated with the program for years. They were all asked to make large contributions toward the new facility, but after the dust settled, the campaign was still short by almost $4 million.

One board member stepped forward and agreed to give an additional $1 million as a challenge if $3 million more could be identified. The executive director agreed, but the major gift staff groaned—they knew that most of the large potential donors had already been solicited. They used the challenge to raise another $1.5 million from lower-level donors but ended up over $1 million short of the goal.

The project had to be reduced from its original plans to meet the lower budget amount available, which annoyed the early donors and supporters. The challenge donor was also irritated but finally agreed to make good on his $1 million challenge match, even though all the terms weren't met. The organization sacrificed both the goodwill of early supporters and the long-term support of the match-giver by agreeing to terms that it couldn't meet.

Board and Staff Roles in Major Gift Fundraising

The Move to Staff-Driven Major Gift Fundraising

The involvement of volunteers and board members is crucial to the success of major gift fundraising. Some organizations, especially those that have been asking for large gifts for a long period of time, are very dependent on volunteer leadership in their major gift programs. The Ivy League advancement offices, for instance, used to rely heavily on a class agent system, in which certain members of each alumni class would press others in their class for a major gift, usually based on the five-year class reunion cycle. Each class would reliably come up with gifts based on the skill and determination of the class agent. Not much staff support was required, and fundraising costs were kept to a minimum.

This model was copied successfully in many institutions and still produces wonderful results today. In some volunteer-driven organizations, board members and other volunteers take prospect names, make the calls, and tell the staff what they've raised when it's all over. Within the past decade or so, however, changing roles, the need for more and bigger gifts, and the lack of volunteer time and commitment have all contributed to a shift in major gift work, from dependence on volunteers to dependence on paid professional staff.

Often volunteers do not have the time, focus, and resources to commit to tracking down a major gift prospect that paid staff members can summon up. The increasingly aggressive fundraising goals of many nonprofit campaigns have contributed to the need for more, bigger, and more complicated fundraising drives. Volunteers may be less willing to board a plane on the East Coast to meet with a major prospect on his schedule in a conference room on the West Coast. Professional staff members have become more adept at developing the long-term relationships that result in larger gifts. In sum, most major gift programs are now run by professional staff with ongoing support from volunteers who remain committed to the success of the organization.

RULES OF THE ROAD

If the donor agrees to the ask amount too quickly, you haven't asked for enough.

Combining Resources for the Best Impact

This is not to say that staff can do it all. Often the most difficult fundraising scenarios arise when the board or the executive director turns all the fundraising over to the advancement staff and steps back, saying, in effect, "You are the professionals, you go do it." Even when major gift staff members are incredibly motivated and talented, it still takes a team effort to raise the money.

What is the proper role for each member of the team? Often this varies from one institution to the next and can depend on the nonprofit's fundraising history, board relations, the strength and experience of the staff, and the number of prospects who have to be reached (see Exhibit 3.4 for recommended roles).

Most staff members are comfortable handling the operational and support side of the major gift effort, including prospect tracking, rating, research, call preparation, proposal writing, and recognition plans. Staff also must be capable of making personal calls and asking for money. Many volunteers still enjoy the personal face-to-face meetings that usually are required to bring in the biggest gifts. These standardized roles leave some room in the middle to determine who makes the appointment, who takes what role in the call, and who handles the follow-up to close the gift. With good communication and a little flexibility, a team approach can be negotiated that serves all parties well.

The balance between staff and volunteer roles often is arrived at through trial and error, and the arrival of new personnel, a new CEO, or new volunteer leadership can require some adjustment to the equation. When all is said and done, the approach that works best is the one that produces the best results in the most efficient way for the nonprofit.

EXHIBIT 3.4

Volunteer and Staff Roles in Major Gift Fundraising

Volunteers

- Review lists of prospects; identify and rate potential donors.

- Open door to prospect with a call or letter.

- Accompany staff, executive director, or other volunteers on call.

- Take part in the call by making the case or making the ask.

- Follow up with prospect to close the gift if needed.

- Thank donors with personal call or letter.

- Participate in recognition events.

- Make a gift!

Major Gift Staff Members

- Prepare lists of prospects for review by volunteers.

- Track prospect names, information, and ratings.

- Prepare or present prospect research to volunteers.

- Make qualifying calls on prospects to determine interest level.

- Prepare volunteers and/or executive director for calls.

- Accompany volunteers and/or executive director on calls.

- Make calls alone on prospects as appropriate to ask for gifts.

- Prepare proposals, letters, and documents needed for solicitation.

- Keep lines of communication open with prospect.

- Follow up to close gift as needed.

- Oversee gift receipt, accounting, and acknowledgment processes.

- Thank donor personally, by phone or letter.

EXHIBIT 3.4 CONTINUED

- Thank volunteer personally.

- Implement recognition and stewardship plans.

Volunteers and Staff Together

- Prioritize prospects based on capacity and readiness.

- Assign dollar level for the solicitation (rating).

- Select team members to call on prospects.

- Prepare for call by assigning role to each team member.

- Conduct calls on prospects.

- Agree on follow-up action to close gift.

- Communicate any additional contacts with prospects.

- Assess results, review roles, adjust as needed.

In a staff-driven program, it is the responsibility of staff members to outline the activities of volunteer fundraisers and provide in-house support for all of their work with donors. Sometimes a consultant also can provide this type of operational support. Volunteers and board members usually are best managed by adhering to a job description, meeting often, and creating an environment where communication between staff and volunteers is easy and comfortable. Nothing is more embarrassing than for a staff member to find out that a volunteer has already approached a prospect before the strategic elements of the call have been hashed out. In many cases, this type of rush to solicit can cause money to be left on the table, a loss for both the organization and the volunteer.

The job description for fundraising volunteers should be written and given out to all volunteers at the time they are recruited. Typical job description components include:

- Size and duration of the fundraising drive

- The length of the term the volunteer will serve

IN THE REAL WORLD

Staff Limitations

One successful environmental nonprofit raised millions of dollars a year by counting on the excellent fundraising skills of the CEO, a charismatic and driven leader. He assumed that if his work could be multiplied—if advancement staff members could make the same number of prospect calls that he made per month—then the nonprofit could raise two or three times the money currently being raised. He called the staff together and outlined the new policy.

Six months later, the results were terribly disappointing. Only a few new donors had been added to the organization, and their gifts were significantly lower than the CEO had expected. What had gone wrong?

The chief advancement office outlined the problem. Given the CEO's high visibility in the region, donors with the potential to make seven-figure gifts all wanted to be called on by him. In addition, most of the region's wealthy donors had already been identified and cultivated by the CEO, leaving only smaller donors for the staff to call on. The CEO's success was actually limiting the capability of his staff to raise new major gifts.

Once the problem was recognized, the group devised new strategies to raise new major gifts. Staff members enhanced their research capabilities to find new donors, mounted a new national fundraising effort, and began to visit top prospects with board members, to slowly "wean" them from always having to be seen by the CEO. Within several years, fundraising had reached new heights.

- Name and title of the volunteer position and the fundraising committee

- Activities spelled out, that is, the volunteer will make three calls per month on prospects assigned by the campaign chair

- Whom the volunteer will report to and take assignments from

- The number and frequency of meetings that the volunteer is expected to attend

- Any expectation that the volunteer will attend a training session

- Any expectation that the volunteer will make a gift

Fundraising volunteer management requires a combination of patience, assertiveness, organizational skills, and follow-up. Weekly or monthly committee meetings can help avoid problems and strategize solutions. Most staff also e-mail, call, or visit volunteers individually (in addition to group meetings) to keep them posted on overall progress and support their calls. In addition, volunteer chairs can be very helpful in promoting good communication, prospect activity, and pushing the number of calls made. Having to report in front of peers on progress (or the lack thereof) is a tried and true method for increasing the activity levels of hesitant volunteers.

Summary

Successful major gift work is often the product of board commitment, leadership, and active involvement. Assess the potential ability of your board members to give or get major gifts before beginning your fundraising drive. Adding board members, changing nominating procedures, and implementing training programs are all options for improving board involvement in a major gift effort.

Many boards focus on fundraising through a give-or-get policy. Giving higher-level gifts can be encouraged by a variety of sight-raising techniques, which build momentum and support for major gift fundraising efforts. Challenges and matching gifts are also a method of promoting contributions at a new higher level for the organization.

Advancement staff members and fundraising volunteers should formulate a team approach to soliciting major gifts. Although specific roles can vary from one organization to another, both sides should agree on their roles, practice good communication, and remain flexible in order to meet the needs of the organization and maximize the efficiency of their fundraising efforts.

CHAPTER 4

Making the Case for a Major Gift

After reading this chapter you will be able to:

- Make the case for your organization
- Create materials that motivate donors
- Develop strategies that bring in larger gifts

Making the Case

Making the case is the term development people use for the argument for why a donor should support a certain cause or organization. For most donors, the case is the key not only to the decision to make a gift, but it influences the size of the gift as well. As we saw in Chapter 1, a donor may give to a nonprofit for a variety of reasons, but most donors give at the outset because they support the mission and goals of the organization. It stands to reason that if the donor has the capacity to make a major gift, then the case must be made not only for why the donor should support the nonprofit but why a large gift is called for.

In the past, many nonprofits were relatively unsophisticated at marketing themselves. They assumed that anyone who is a good and thoughtful person will intuitively understand the need for, and importance of, the work that the organization did in the community. These days, given the plethora of choices that an active phil-anthropist has to make a meaningful contribution to the welfare of others, it is im-portant to create a unique and lasting impression on would-be contributors. Doing this calls for a more thoughtful and targeted approach to marketing the work of the nonprofit organization.

Focus on Elements That Distinguish Your Nonprofit from Others

The secret to making a strong case with prospective donors is to select and build on elements that illustrate the unique nature of the organization's work and its out-comes. This case can be presented visually through brochures or verbally through conversations, or it can be illustrated more personally by having the prospective donor tour the nonprofit's site. However it is presented, the case must be com-pelling, timely, and tied to the overall mission and vision of the nonprofit.

Conceptually, the case should arise from the nature of the work being done by the organization. Analyzing the answers to basic questions about your nonprofit, such as what services you provide, whom you serve, how you provide services, and why the services are needed, can help you to arrive at the components of your case. You may wish to involve a communications consultant, or perhaps a volunteer experienced in public relations, to help ascertain how your organization can best pre-sent itself to potential donors.

Education, healthcare, social services, and the arts are basic elements of much of the work of nonprofits in our communities, but they can be described in detail to help a prospective supporter understand the nature of the services better. Convene an appropriate planning group and ask members questions like these:

- What is the nature of the work of your nonprofit?

- What services and programs are provided?

- What kind of outreach do you provide in the community?

- Who uses the organization's services?

- What are the outcomes for the organization's efforts?

- How can these outcomes be illustrated or measured?

Your knowledge of *who* uses the services your organization provides can offer useful material for building the case. Is there a profile available of the typical person who comes to your nonprofit for assistance? Can you gather basic demographic information about visitors, students, patients, or other service users? Are there people who fit your user profile who can't get to use your services because of your organization's funding limitations? Research and data, along with personal profiles, can help you to define and analyze your service population.

Questioning *why* a service is needed also helps to refine points for your case. Have there been cuts in federal dollars that used to be available? Is the need for the service growing? Is there a special need in your community for the services you provide? In order to create a better sense of why investing in your programs is so important, think about how to link your organization's purpose to the needs for these services.

The final building block for your case is to *differentiate* your organization from others like it. Are there programs that are unusual or unique? Can you measure the success rate of your programs against those of other groups like yours? Are there ways that your programs have already improved the quality of life in your community? Are there other indicators that might illustrate or measure the progress that has been attained?

Review your mission and goals to make sure that your case presentation fits into the overall purpose of the organization as stated by your leaders. If your organizational mission is to alleviate hunger, then build your case on why hunger is a problem and how you propose to alleviate it. To illustrate the need in your community, you also can develop profiles on who is a victim of hunger and how they were helped by your services.

Identify One or Two Themes in Making Your Case

In the world of nonprofit fundraising, focus is often the key to success. In order to create strong and memorable materials to help you present the case for your institution, review the elements you have used to create your case and focus on one or two specific themes. These themes can then form the nucleus of the supporting material, both print and electronic, that you develop to present your case to potential donors.

Select a Compelling Theme to Make Your Case

Creating a compelling case can help to attract major donors. A popular example is the economic development theme, which can be applied to a variety of nonprofits.

An art museum had traditionally developed its case based on its central mission, that of providing leadership and education in the arts. In an attempt to attract new corporate donations, however, the museum chose to make the case for its new fundraising effort based on the economic development that it provided to the community. It even commissioned an economic impact study to measure its effect on the region.

The economic impact study showed the number of visitors who came to the city to see museum exhibits, the amount of additional discretionary dollars these visitors spent, and the overall dollar impact the museum had on the community.

The statistics positively influenced local corporate and civic leaders, many of whom had never before supported the museum. The drive was a big success and attracted new major donors to the museum.

Thematic elements selected to make the case can be simple or complex, as long as they communicate a strong sense of why the donor should support the institution (see Exhibit 4.1).

The best themes are authentic to the organization, carry emotional impact, and illustrate the meeting of a need. Thematic elements that provide poignancy, add urgency, and tell personal stories add drama to the case. A strong theme will always be conceptually grounded in the mission and vision of the organization, whether it is used for marketing or fundraising purposes.

Testing your organization's case and themes with external constituents can be a helpful step in determining their efficacy. Marketing and PR firms can provide access to focus groups for testing materials and themes. You may want to provide your own testing groups selected from potential donors, current donors, and past donors.

EXHIBIT 4.1

Example of Effective Themes

- A university creates profiles of prominent alumni to illustrate how its successful graduates give back to their community.

- A museum highlights programs for schoolchildren that it developed to offset cuts in the arts made by the local school district.

- A high school features the courses in technology training it offers at night for adult students.

- A community shelter emphasizes its program to combat local street crime by providing counseling for substance abusers.

- A youth group focuses attention on its work with providing adult mentors to inner-city youth to help them go straight.

- A literacy program that tutors adults and children from the same homes profiles success stories in a series of ads.

Consider testing two or three potential themes against each other to determine which one elicits the stronger response.

Making the Case for a Major Gift

Once the organization identifies its basic case and themes, additional components can be built into the case to encourage donors to make a major contribution to the cause. Donors will consider several key questions during the course of the cultivation and solicitation process for a major gift. Several factors can influence the size of a potential gift:

- How will making a major gift allow the organization to offer more or better services?

- How will making a major gift make an impact on the organization, the community, and the cause?

- How will other people important to the donor (spouse, family, board members, peers, business colleagues, and friends) perceive this gift?

- What is urgent about making this gift now?

A case framed around these issues can form the basis for supporting materials, such as brochures, proposals, and letters, which will be used with prospective donors. These issues also can be addressed personally in cultivation events, face-to-face meetings, and small get-togethers with potential prospects. With larger groups, the case for making a major gift can be integrated into fundraising events, speeches, and video presentations.

It is important to develop your key themes and case materials before launching a major gift effort. If you haven't determined how additional funding will allow your organization to better provide services, then you probably aren't ready to ask for major gifts. You must be ready to articulate the potential outcomes of having more money to invest in the nonprofit's program, capital construction, or endowment (whatever area you are fundraising for), as part of making the case for a major gift.

The Donor as Investor

It may be helpful to think of the donor as an investor, a person of wealth who is studying an array of investment choices, which could range from mutual funds to hedge funds. The investor will want to understand the impact, the risks, the returns, and the inner workings of each investment vehicle (i.e., of the nonprofit) before making a decision. He will ask for the prospectus (think of this as your giving brochures

 LIVE & LEARN

What's Wrong with That?

A retired political operative was helping the development office as a volunteer on the Major Gifts Committee. After reviewing the prospect list, she selected a very wealthy potential donor as her prospect. Unfortunately, several weeks later, the prospect was indicted for fraud. The major gifts officer called her to cancel the appointment with the prospect. "Why should we cancel?" the volunteer asked in a surprised tone of voice. "He's only been indicted, not convicted!"

TIPS & TECHNIQUES

5 Ways to Make Your Case Stand Out

1. Introduce the basics briefly: the history of your organization, what services you provide, whom you serve, and why the services are needed.

2. Focus on what makes you different from other groups that provide similar services.

3. Develop personal profiles into stories that feature successful outcomes.

4. Illustrate the impact more funding will have in providing better services.

5. Create a sense of urgency about why more funding is needed now.

as well as gift investment policies, naming and recognition opportunities, and stewardship policies). He probably will want to know who is running the fund (your board, investment consultants, and executive staff) and who else has invested with you (other major gift donors, board giving).

Taking into account the opinion of others—or their perceived opinions—is often part of the donor's internal, unspoken understanding of her place in her social, business, and family networks. Peer opinion and support can be made part of the case in subtle ways, such as selecting who goes on the call. A prospect probably will view a cultivation call made by the chair of the board, for instance, as placing her higher in the pecking order than one made by a low-level staff member.

Another way to manage the peer perception issue during a solicitation call is to bring along a list of the names and gift levels of other major contributors. (Be sure you have each donor's permission to use his or her name and gift amount before doing this.) The prospect can thus compare herself to other donors, many of whom presumably will be her peers, as she considers various gift amounts.

Finally, it is important to address the urgency of making a contribution to the cause when making the case for a major gift. A sense of urgency can arise from the work of the organization itself; if, for instance, a homeless shelter needs to expand, then a case can be made that people are homeless, winter is coming on, and therefore an immediate solution to the problem must be found. Urgency also can arise from the need to gain access to a site, fulfill a promise, or meet a special set of needs.

Placing emphasis on campaign timelines also increases the urgency quotient. A capital campaign might need to be completed by next year, due to the need to match a federal grant by a certain deadline. Fundraising challenges can help to focus donors on a set timeline for making gifts. A sense of urgency helps to build momentum, creates demand for more prospect and volunteer activity, and ultimately helps to close more gifts.

Communicating the Case: Materials That Motivate Donors

A great deal of time, effort, and money is spent on materials that make the case to potential donors by nonprofits. Most of these pieces are not terribly effective because they fail to focus on elements that differentiate the organization from others that provide similar services. Developing communication materials and strategies that effectively educate, involve, and motivate donors is an important component of any major gift program.

Who Should Develop Major Gift Materials?

Many nonprofits use outside vendors to help them develop materials to use in major gift work. This is especially true if a major gift program will be part of a larger capital campaign, which usually requires additional PR and marketing support. The vendor can be an advertising or PR firm, a graphics and design firm, or a Web services provider, depending on the type of support required.

Selecting a vendor can be time-consuming. Sometimes board members have recommendations for vendors they use in their own business relationships. Perhaps you have a volunteer or board member who specializes in these types of services, who can offer them free or at a lower cost. If you use a fundraising consultant, ask for recommendations on providers who have experience with nonprofit fundraising work.

RULES OF THE ROAD

What to tell a donor who offers a bequest when you asked for a major gift:
"Give with a warm hand."

Peers at other nonprofits also can recommend experienced providers of graphic design, Web, and printing services.

External vendors have some advantages when it comes to producing materials for use in advancement. They may have access to top designers, and for major gift work you will want a piece that is of high quality. An outsider may approach your organization with fresh eyes and thus be more able to develop new approaches to how you differentiate yourself and market your strengths. In most cases, however, an outside PR or design firm is more expensive than writing and producing materials in-house.

If your organization has internal PR, communications, or publications staff, consider using them to develop your major gift materials. Internal people often have a deeper knowledge of the organization and can identify themes and "tell the story" more effectively than outside consultants. In-house staff members usually are less expensive than outside providers, although they may lack the design sophistication needed for materials aimed at top prospects. Using in-house staff members may also affect the production timetable, so be sure to determine ahead of time if they have the time and capacity to handle your needs.

Printed Materials

Printed materials, including letters, brochures, proposals, donor lists, and annual reports, are all widely used in major gift fundraising. Printed materials give the user some key advantages: A prospect can retain them and pass them around to family members or other decision makers; they are often very attractively designed; and they can present a strong case for the cause being presented. The pros and cons for using printed materials versus electronic formats are highlighted in Exhibit 4.2.

TIPS & TECHNIQUES

When Using an Outside PR or Design Firm to Produce Materials

- Have them spend time with the organization to learn about the services provided.

- Give them the opportunity to meet people who have benefited from the services the organization provides.

- Have them meet with staff members who will be using the materials.

- Give the advancement director input with the PR firm and sign off responsibility on the materials produced.

- Test market potential themes and approaches using focus groups.

- Pin down costs for photography, paper, and printing in advance.

Yet printing, paper, and mailing costs have all increased exponentially, while newer, electronic communication formats provide information at a lower cost per person. Using video, computer-generated, or PowerPoint presentations can give the organization a more cutting-edge image. Electronic formats also provide an easier, cheaper means of updating information. Perhaps the main reason why printed materials are still so popular is that people expect to see them—and not only prospects! Volunteers, board members, CEOs, and advancement staff in many organizations don't feel that they are ready to talk to prospects until they have an information packet or brochure in hand.

Many experienced solicitors feel that this dependence on packets and fancy brochures is misplaced. The old adage that *people give to people* comes to mind; prospective donors often are more interested in who calls on them, what rationale they give for making a gift, and how the gift will have an impact on the cause being addressed than in the printed materials that solicitors leave behind. Although it may be necessary to create an attractive brochure, don't rely too heavily on printed materials to sway a donor.

EXHIBIT 4.2

Printed Materials versus Electronic Communication

Advantages of Using Printed Materials

- Printed materials have more appeal to traditional, older donors who have been raised to value books, letters, and newspapers.

- They can be saved and circulated to other decision makers, including family members, foundation boards, and corporate giving committees.

- They can make a strong impact visually and emotionally through well-designed layout, strong copy, and high-quality photos.

- They can be distributed through many channels: sent through the mail, given out at events, or delivered in personal calls.

- They are still the gold standard for marketing for nonprofits and often are expected by volunteers, board members, donors, and prospects.

Advantages of Using Electronic Means of Communication

- Electronic formats can appear more modern, more technologically advanced, and give the organization a cutting-edge appeal.

- They may be more appealing to younger donors.

- They can be less expensive to produce and distribute.

- They can be less expensive to reformat and update.

- They can be easily personalized for large numbers of prospects.

- They provide a kind of immediacy and interactivity that print communication lacks.

Beyond brochures, simple printed materials like proposals, letters, and notes can play an important role in the process of cultivating major gift prospects. Because of the ease and popularity of newer methods of communication like e-mail, the value of a small, handwritten note has risen exponentially. The act of dropping a personal, handwritten note to thank a prospect for her time and interest, once taken for granted, has now become a sign of significant attention.

The Failure of Rainbow Brite

A large successful nonprofit with a new marketing director was preparing for a national major gifts effort. The marketing director hired an outside design and printing firm that was more familiar with corporate clients than with nonprofits. The organization signed a generous six-figure contract with the design firm to produce a brochure that was supposed to highlight key themes to make the nonprofit's case with high-level donors.

The project ended up a total disaster. The advancement team was never consulted on the elements of the brochure; no market research with donors or prospects was done; and the tone and image created for the brochure were at odds with the organization's historic mission and purpose. Due to poor design, the thematic elements that were supposed to make the case disappeared in a blur of colorful tabs. The resulting piece, printed in bold primary colors, came to be dubbed "Rainbow Brite" by the major gift staff members, who refused to use it in their work with prospects.

Ultimately the organization wasted a lot of money, time, and effort on a piece that failed to represent its basic values and didn't meet the needs of its audience.

Proposals and letters that show signs of real personalization (as opposed to word-processed changes in salutations) are becoming rarer in our electronic age. Ironically, giving *actual* personal attention to a prospect—as opposed to mass computerized "personalization"—has become an attractive selling point with wealthy donors, most of whom are sophisticated enough to recognize the difference between multiple fonts and a personally signed letter.

Electronic Materials

Many people of wealth now receive so many appeals for funds that it has become a challenge to stand out in the crowd. Fun, attractive, and cutting-edge electronic presentations can help get a prospect's attention. Fly-through computer graphics are being used to show off new sites and construction projects; slick fundraising videos can be downloaded from Web sites; and online fundraising appeals are

Making the Case: Using a Brochure Effectively

An effective brochure doesn't cost hundreds of thousands of dollars and need to be 30 pages of full color. One nonprofit made an effective case for its need for an expanded building with a four-page color brochure that they produced in-house. This is how they did it.

Their brochure was attractive in its design, used a good-quality paper stock, and measured 9-x-11-inches when folded, so that it stood out from other pieces. The front cover featured attractive artistic elements taken from the nonprofit's logo and announced the campaign's name and their goal.

The first page featured a brief letter from the board chair, outlining the need for the new facility and identifying two main themes, education and economic development. The second page carried highlighted quotes from civic leaders about the economic impact of the organization's work, the projected future economic impact after the expansion, and attendance figures that supported the need for expansion.

The inside pages also featured attractive pictures of children visiting the current facility to support the educational theme. Quotes from teachers praised the ongoing success of the nonprofit's outreach programs.

The back page carried all the giving information, including naming opportunities with prices and the names of the volunteer fundraising committee members, and briefly highlighted different ways of giving.

Some brochures were mailed ahead to secure appointments with major gift prospects. Volunteers used others on calls when asking for gifts. Donors loved the simple format, and found the brochure both easy to read and comprehensible. All the money was raised within two years.

e-mailed to millions of supporters. Electronic communication has reached a new level of acceptance and, more important, is producing results.

Plan to use the means and methods of communication that are most likely to be appreciated by the prospects for your organization. If your major gift prospects are mostly under the age of 55 and like to be seen as hip, then by all means use the latest in computerized graphics to help wow them with your technological savvy. If the biggest donor to your organization is likely to be an 80-year-old widow who sends everything she gets in the mail to her lawyer and accountant, you probably need to take a more conservative approach.

Consider ways to tastefully integrate the methods of communication that are most likely to be useful in your major gift efforts (see Exhibit 4.3). If you start with an expensive printed piece, for instance, plan to reuse the full-color photographs on your Web site and in your monthly e-mail newsletter. If you create a new video to use at your annual fundraising event, post it on your Web site after the event and refer visitors to it through direct mail.

PowerPoint presentations are inexpensive to produce and can provide a strong visual impression when used during a solicitation call. Videos can pull the heartstrings, providing an emotional base for a strong cultivation event or visit. PowerPoint presentations and videos can be reproduced inexpensively on CDs and left with prospects after a call, just as brochures can. Nonprofits now find it easy to produce videos and PowerPoint presentations that are individualized with the prospect's name, ask amount, and naming opportunity.

You will want to develop a strong visual and thematic identity for your organization that is consistent from one means of communication to another; repeating logos, colors, and design elements can be helpful. Take care to keep on target with your message—don't develop one set of themes for your written case and create another entirely different approach for your video. Donors and prospects should be able to recognize your organization immediately, whether the medium is print or electronic. Repeating thematic and design elements in different media can help to create a consistent case for your organization.

 RULES OF THE ROAD

Don't mention a donor's recent major gift in front of his wife or grown children unless you are absolutely sure they know about it.

EXHIBIT 4.3

Materials Needed in a Major Gift Program

- One major full-color printed brochure (12 to 14 pages) for use in face-to-face meetings with major gift prospects

- One small brochure (three-fold), with the same design elements as the larger one, used to mail when requesting appointments and as a handout

- One short (5- to 6-minute) video featuring stories of people who have used the services provided by your organization; to be used at events and left with prospects after a meeting

- One PowerPoint presentation (10 minutes) that can be used at events or in conference rooms with prospects

- One proposal template each for corporation, foundation, and individual prospects

- Web site that features video and themes from the brochure

- Printed folder with pockets that can be individualized for each prospect (Use it for materials created in-house, including proposals, letters, donor lists, recognition and naming opportunities, press releases, etc.)

Strategies that Help to Motivate Gifts

The prospective donor learns a great deal about an organization from sources other than a fundraising brochure, an in–house video, and a meeting with staff or volunteers. Although the fundraising staff can control some of the media and message that gets to the donor, other means of communication have to be coordinated to help the organization promote its case effectively. Often this requires communication and planning across different departments. Researching and tracking personal information about the prospect also can help to target a message that will motivate the donor to become more involved with the organization.

Coordinating PR and Communication Strategy

One approach to promoting an effective case is to create a strategic communications plan across the organization. Doing this allows the nonprofit to define and deliver a carefully crafted message, or series of messages, as effectively and as efficiently as possible (see Exhibit 4.4). Staff members from the departments of fundraising, PR, and publications should all participate; include all groups that provide or produce information for external audiences. You may want to begin with an informal audit of the communications vehicles that currently are being used, identifying what is being sent out, whom it goes to, and what the purpose for each piece is.

Defining the message, the audience, and the media will help the organization to coordinate and target external communications efforts. Doing this in turn helps support the work of the major gift staff, who are working with a much smaller and focused audience of identified prospects. A coordinated communications effort improves the chances of major gift prospects receiving information from various sources that is integrated, stays on point, and reinforces earlier communications, all of which is highly desirable in order to raise money.

Targeting Donor Involvement Through Prospect Research

The potential for researching and tracking prospects electronically allows organizations to target prospects more individually than has been possible in the past. Advertisers have become much more sophisticated at identifying the needs, buying habits, and spending patterns of customers; many retailers now keep a record of what each customer buys by tracking individual e-mail addresses, telephone numbers, and mailing addresses. They use this information to predict customer habits and to offer each customer products they think will fit that individual's needs. Repeat customers of a retail Web site, for instance, find that the site uses their purchase record to predict their interest areas and make suggestions about what they might want to buy.

In a similar manner, by using information that you have on file for each prospect, you may be able to work with that prospect in a more personalized manner. The

EXHIBIT 4.4

Matrix for a Strategic Communications Plan

Medium	Audience	Message	Distribution	Desired Action
Printed 12-page Brochure Developed by PR firm	500 major gift Prospects	Makes the case: develops 2 themes, quality of education, & economic impact	Mailed first class with letter from chairman of the board	Accept an appointment with a volunteer and/or major gifts staff member when called; become familiar with case
5-minute Video Developed by same PR firm, uses colors, design from brochure	Attendees at annual black tie fundraising dinner (includes 50 of top 100 prospects)	Case: Builds on same two themes but adds more emotion with interviews and profiles	Viewed at dinner; then posted on Web site and reproduced on CDs for use on calls	Build emotional support, show outcomes of organization's work; talk to friends about the organization
PowerPoint Developed in-house, picks up themes from brochure, video	Use on face-to-face calls with top 100 prospects (bring along already loaded on a laptop)	Case: Outlines case, emphasizes financial need, impact of gift, and giving options	Each prospect gets an individualized presentation based on his rating; a copy is left behind after the call	Make a gift of $25,000 to $1,000,000 depending on capacity, interest, and rating
Newsletter Produced quarterly in-house, repeats same themes and design	Entire mailing list: All donors at all levels, boards, prospects, volunteers, and staff	Tells stories and highlights programs that support themes; devotes one issue to each theme	Mailed bulk and posted on Web site	Make annual gift to support operations, reinforces information for major gift prospects
New Print Ad Campaign Designed and placed by PR firm	All readers in the region; focus is on corporate, civic, business decision makers	Focus on theme of how organization supports economic development in region	Series of 4 ads run sequentially in daily paper and business journal	Gain corporate sponsorships, build support from public sources

TIPS & TECHNIQUES

How to Combine Prospect Research with Target Marketing

- Identify current donors who have given major gifts to other nonprofits that provide similar services; call on them personally to discuss increasing their support for your organization.

- Locate current donors to your organization who sit on the board of foundations that give in your area of need; call and ask them to help you with preparing a proposal to their foundation.

- Locate current donors to your organization who work at corporations that might become prospective supporters; ask them to help you contact the corporate giving person and to come with you on the call.

- Send personal letters to current donors who have the potential to give larger gifts, inviting them to tour your facility.

- Target invitations to events by age, giving younger donors an opportunity to network with supporters in their own age group.

- Invite older prospects to take part in a volunteer activity at your nonprofit to begin their involvement.

end result is that your organization will be able to make its case more effectively to each prospect. Some organizations are reluctant to use these marketing techniques in the nonprofit sector, viewing them as slick, intrusive, or privacy-invading. With appropriate controls and good taste, however, you can apply these techniques in a manner that fits the style of your organization.

Tracking and coordinating information on each prospect requires gathering information in an accurate and cost-effective manner to begin. Prospect research data can come from one of several sources (see section on prospect research in Chapter 2). Electronic prospect research companies are often the most efficient means of compiling and tracking personalized information to help you target your marketing approach with prospects.

"Data mining," the latest term for electronic prospect research, allows your research capacity to be increased by searching multiple databases very quickly. The information you receive on names already in your database can help you identify past giving to other organizations, find indicators of wealth, unearth connections to foundations and corporations, establish links to other major donors to your institution, and help you to assign a potential rating for a gift. By mining additional information, such as age, donations made to public officials, and board affiliations, you can match potential donors up with appropriate contacts from your organization.

Strategies to Engage Major Donors

It is very rare for a prospect to make a large gift without having some prior interaction with the charitable organization she is giving to. A few odd cases of surprise bequests sometimes make the news, but the very rarity of these gifts makes them newsworthy. Most donors are knowledgeable about a nonprofit and are involved in some way with furthering their efforts before making the commitment of a large gift. An analysis of how your organization provides opportunities for engagement with prospective donors can help lead to larger gifts later in the relationship (see Exhibit 4.5).

The first level of engagement with the prospective major donor often occurs through some initial action on the part of the donor herself. This is why current

---

EXHIBIT 4.5

Engaging Prospects: Ideas for Involvement

- Ask prospects to complete a survey or questionnaire.

- Request their critique on a brochure or Web site.

- Invite them to make a site visit.

- Ask them to volunteer or join a committee.

- Have a current supporter invite them to attend an event as their guest.

- Ask them to serve on an advisory board.

- Invite them to provide services for your organization.

- Request an interview with them for an article in your newsletter.

- Plan to give them an award or honor at your next big event.

donor databases should be run through a good electronic screening program—you never know when the last $50 check came from someone who gave $20 million to his alma mater last year. Many advancement professionals set up a comprehensive plan to track every contact made with the organization, from visitors on site to visitors on the Web site. Contacts should be tracked with codes showing how the name entered your database, so that later you can reconstruct how the prospect entered the system.

Once a donor is identified as being capable of making a larger gift, through prospect research, electronic screening, or peer referral, make a plan for how that prospect can become more involved in the work of the nonprofit. This plan can be adjusted according to how the prospect name arrived in your database. If the prospect arrived through a Web site hit, for instance, you might consider constructing an interactive e-mail exchange, using a questionnaire or market survey instrument designed to elicit a response.

Those who sent you a check in the mail might be sent a print version of the same survey. Ideally you want to get donors to respond to you, to exchange information, and to share more insight on their interests, habits, and giving patterns. After the initial exchange is made, it is easier for you to visit prospects, invite them to events, ask them to volunteer, or simply stay in communication through a newsletter.

There are other strategies to encourage donor engagement for those people who have not had prior contact with your organization. Ask 10 donors or members of your board to give you the names of five people each whom they know who could be helpful in a major gifts effort, either as donors or volunteers. Invite those 50 people to your organization for a site visit. Set up a two-hour program in which they can learn about your organization's needs, take a tour, and meet with some of the people your services have helped. Ask your donor or board contact to make the follow-up call to help get the prospects to attend and, if possible, to agree to meet their friends there.

Outreach events can bring new people aboard in a similar manner. Ask a current donor or board member to host an event for your organization in a unique home or special site, such as a boardroom, that will attract people who aren't familiar with your cause. Then employ the same strategy of having your inner circle identify five friends whom they can invite to the event. Be sure your inner circle members will also be there to help support the cause. Then plan appropriate follow-up with promising attendees.

Summary

Motivating donors to make major gifts starts with building an effective case. Focus on one or two themes to help differentiate your organization from others that provide similar services. A compelling case includes what additional services are needed, why they are needed, how additional funds will be used, and what impact a major gift will have on solving the issues at hand. Making the case can be done effectively through a variety of print and electronic materials, from brochures to videos to personal letters.

Your organization's message should be consistent throughout all of your communication efforts. Coordinate across departments and divisions to create a unified plan in communicating with external constituencies. Donors respond to real needs, stated in a compelling manner, communicated effectively through a variety of media.

Using prospect research to target communications to a donor's specific interests or demographic can help a nonprofit market its needs most effectively to those who have the greatest capacity to help. Engaging donors personally through interactive communication, volunteer activities, and on-site visits is an effective way to motivate larger gifts.

CHAPTER 5

Cultivation of Major Gift Prospects

After reading this chapter you will be able to:

- Make a qualifying call
- Build relationships through cultivation
- Talk about money with a prospect

Opening the Door to Cultivation

Wealthy people have developed myriad ways to protect themselves from being harassed by salespeople, charities, and needy relatives. Often, even if you are quite certain that a prospect would be interested in giving to your organization, the biggest problem is getting in the door. It is one thing to have a name on your list of major gift prospects; it is quite another to meet that person face-to-face and begin to develop a relationship. And meeting face-to-face is a required first step in major gifts work. Several ways to accomplish this goal have proven successful, but you may develop your own special skills in this area.

Initial Contact: Getting in the Door

Getting in the door means more than dropping off a case summary with the prospect's secretary or mailing a brochure to an office address. The goal is to make a meaningful, personal contact, whether that is by e-mail, phone, or preferably, face-to-face. This can be a difficult goal to reach in today's world of layers of protection; many people of wealth surround themselves with defenses, from personal security teams to answering machines. It comes as a relief to find the occasional entrepreneur who still answers his own phone and greets his visitors in person.

Getting in the door to see wealthy potential donors has become a time-consuming activity. Realize before you begin that some prospects, even those whom you have reason to think might be interested in your cause, are just not going to be approachable. Decide how many tries you want to make—four or five is a reasonable limit—and give up and move on to others who are more accessible.

Successful sales managers teach their staff that there is a whole universe of likely prospects out there; the ones who are worth your time and energy are the subset of that universe whom you can reach, whom you can develop a relationship with, and who show interest in your product. There are many others who aren't worth your time and energy. Be prepared to cross names off your list if they aren't productive after reasonable efforts and move on.

Given that all your efforts won't pan out, some prospects are worth greater efforts than others. The relative wealth of a prospect is always a factor, while philanthropic intent in your area of service is a key criterion. Thus a prospect who is a billionaire, gives away millions annually through his foundation, and shows interest in the topic of adult literacy is definitely worth pursuing if you are operating in that field.

The best way to set up a call is to have someone the prospective donor knows and trusts open the door for the meeting. This can hold true even if the donor is known to the organization and already makes contributions; the added impact of the third-party endorsement makes the donor more likely to respond favorably to the visit. The trusted third party can be a business colleague, a social peer, a friend, a staff member, a family member, or an old classmate. The person who opens the door should be someone who is already familiar with the nonprofit. The door opener does not have to be a major gift donor herself, but she should be a donor who

TIPS & TECHNIQUES

Tips for Getting in the Door

- Send a letter ahead and reference the letter in your call.

- Find a supporter of your organization who knows the prospect; have her call and introduce you.

- Ask the prospect to participate in a study or survey.

- Mention the names of other prospects whom you are meeting with whom this prospect is likely to know.

- Tell the prospect you will be visiting in his city for only one day to create a sense of urgency.

supports the organization within her means. Ideally she will also be passionate and knowledgeable about the cause.

Some volunteers who open doors to prospects enjoy making the resulting call alone, while some prefer to be part of a team, accompanied by a staff member or another volunteer. Others are willing to make the phone call and then hand the meeting off to someone else. It doesn't matter which track is pursued, as long as the volunteers and staff all agree on the course of action ahead of time and the prospect understands just who will participate in the meeting at the time an appointment is set. It can be embarrassing to have the chair of the board tell a Fortune 500 chief executive officer that he will join the meeting and then have him back out at the last minute. Make sure that all calendars are cleared ahead of time.

Qualifying Calls

The purpose of a qualifying call is to assess the prospect's interest, capability, and readiness for making a major gift to the organization.

For the major gift staff member, the first basic step in the cultivation process is conducting the qualifying call. Usually the major gift staff member will place the phone call to the prospect himself, although having a volunteer "open the door" to the prospect can be a useful way to begin the relationship. Some major gift offices

RULES OF THE ROAD

Complaints from donors come in inverse proportion to the size of their gifts.

hire an individual whose job it is to make appointments; a highly skilled appointment setter can save staff time.

Who deserves a qualifying call? In many organizations, the prospect researcher produces names of potential donors who are known as "suspects" until a staff member has the opportunity to meet with them personally. Suspects are initially identified because they have either a connection to the organization or a potential link to wealth (or both). Electronic prospect screening, for instance, can produce a list of potential major gift donors from your organization's own database. This group of names might be linked to your cause through having made small gifts, but prospect screening shows that they have the potential to make larger gifts. Once their names are identified, something has to be done with them—but what? This is where the qualifying call comes into play.

The staff person should be familiar with all the known information about the prospect before placing the call: giving record, prior connections to the nonprofit, family situation, and business role. It is highly likely that at this early phase of the relationship, not all of these factors will be known yet; the point is, however, not to miss information of value that is already in the files.

Assessing the Prospect's Interest and Readiness

The first visit, or qualifying visit, should be viewed as an opportunity to exchange information. The staff member is sharing information about the organization, including mission, vision, needs, and services. She is also listening carefully to understand and assess the donor's level of interest, areas of interest, and possible ways in which she can provide follow-up information. The prospective donor is listening to learn about the organization but is also revealing information through her level of enthusiasm, her questions, and the amount of time she gives to the staff member. If an initial gift is solicited, the response is also a means of assessing the seriousness of the prospect's level of interest. Generally, both parties are offering information, asking questions, and assessing whether they want to follow-up and how.

The staff member should not do all the talking on a qualifying call. The staff member is there to present the organization's case, but she must also listen to the donor and guide the conversational flow with questions suggested by the nature of the conversation. The staff member must remember that she is there to learn all she can about the donor, not inundate the donor with information.

Don't wait to file a written report on each qualifying call—prospect information is easy to forget after 8 or 10 appointments begin to blur together in your head! Keep notes from each call that can be written up at the end of your trip, or use a laptop or a recording device to enter notes right away. Those who follow you will be grateful for a concise, clear report that outlines the visit and the response for the record (see the "Tracking to Stay Focused" section). Of course, each visit should be followed up with a personal note or e-mail, and don't forget to provide any information promised. Keeping the lines of communication open after the visit is one of the key objectives of the qualifying call.

 TIPS & TECHNIQUES

Questions to Ask in a Qualifying Call

- Are you involved with other nonprofits in the community?

- What are your philanthropic priorities?

- What do you already know about our organization?

- Have you ever visited our site? Can I offer you a tour?

- Tell me more about your company/business/work.

- Would you be interested in volunteering in (name a specific) program?

- Can I send you more information on our work in (name a specific) area?

- Would you be willing to make an annual fund contribution to support our ongoing programs?

Assessment of Wealth

Assessing wealth is not always easy or even possible from the visible signs present during a personal meeting with a prospect. Research will have to fill in the gaps. It is always useful to remember that some people, especially those who were brought up in the 1930s during the Depression era, do not "wear" their wealth; they may live quite frugally and appear to exist on modest means. Others live from day to day on multiple lines of credit—that Jaguar in the driveway might be repossessed tomorrow. Do not make the mistake of arriving at quick and superficial judgments about a person's means.

Given that caveat, there are some obvious wealth markers that a major gifts staff member should be on the lookout for (see Exhibit 5.1). Sometimes questions about interests, hobbies, vacations, second homes, education, and family members will help to ascertain wealth, but the savvy donor will hide behind platitudes or even refuse to answer. Because questions about personal matters need to be posed very tactfully, it may be easier to elicit information about the nature of the prospect's business. Many businesspeople and entrepreneurs will discuss their firm's clients, profitability, dividends, and prospects without hesitation. Again, the best advice is to ask questions, let the prospect lead the conversation, listen carefully, and keep your eyes open.

Tracking to Stay Focused

Many organizations develop prospect codes to help them track and sort information gathered from such qualifying meetings. You might learn, for instance, that this prospect is interested in your capital campaign but that it will take at least a year for her to give, because she is heavily involved in her children's school campaign this year. This information can be coded and entered into the development information system so that you or a colleague can bring it up next year when someone goes back to her city.

After the qualifying call, it is important for the staff member to identify "next steps" for the prospect. Many development information systems allow entries with action dates to identify next steps, so that prospects can be pulled by the date that the next step should take place. Prospect tracking system modules can hold up to three or four next steps for each prospect (see Exhibit 5.2).

EXHIBIT 5.1

Wealth Markers (Signs That Prospects MAY Have Personal Wealth)

- Model of car or cars driven

- Type of house, location, and neighborhood

- Existence of second home or vacation homes

- Sports and personal interests, especially those that require expensive equipment or travel (i.e., horses, skiing, car racing, polo, etc.)

- Country clubs, business clubs, or memberships in high-profile organizations

- Travel experiences, especially unusual trips abroad

- Jewelry or expensive clothing

- Known large gifts made to other nonprofits

- Existence of a family foundation or a family corporation

- Type of business, title, level of ownership, and profitability

- Wealthy friends, colleagues, peers, acquaintances

- Private prep schools and/or colleges attended, or children attended

- Willingness to make a gift, preferably at the leadership annual fund level

Most development information systems now have spaces for the entry of additional prospect-related data after a qualifying call. Examples of data entries include: assigned staff manager's name; assigned volunteer's name; projected date of solicitation, ask and expect amount; and area of interest (i.e. endowment, capital, or a specific program). Some institutions enter a total giving capacity that differs from the ask rating; for instance, if a prospect has a family foundation, his long-term giving capacity might be millions, but the first ask is going to be made at $250,000, for an expected gift of $100,000. Usually the major gifts staff member creates and enters this data directly into the information system, although in some offices a data clerk or program coordinator takes over this task.

EXHIBIT 5.2

Examples of Next Steps after a Qualifying Call

1. Mail a package of information on a specific program (with date).

2. Call to invite the prospect to the annual fundraising event (with date).

3. Call to ask the prospect to join the fundraising committee (with date).

4. Follow up to ask for a gift of $50,000 (with date).

Whatever the exact data fields in the information system, if prospects are judged to be a potential major gift donor after the qualification visit, then they should be assigned a gift rating and plan for action. The plan for action should bring the organization closer to realizing a major gift from those prospects. The codes, systems, and next steps with dates attached are all tools that allow the major gift staff member to track, manage, and stay involved with hundreds of prospects at the same time in an organized, efficient, and personalized manner (see Exhibit 5.3).

 LIVE & LEARN

Whose Place Is This, Anyway?

The donor who gave the big gift to name the new building on campus was given many thanks by the university. His name was put up in lights above the door, a bronze plaque recognized his generosity, and a touching dedication ceremony was held. A few months later, though, strange things began to happen.

First, all the trash cans were removed from around the building. Then the furniture began to be rearranged. Finally, a security officer discovered the donor in the building at night carrying out a computer in his arms. "What is going on here?" asked the officer. "Well," the donor replied, "I didn't like the way the trash was out there in front of everyone. And I don't think they laid the furniture out right. And now I need to borrow a computer for my friend. It *is* my building, you know."

EXHIBIT 5.3	
Sample Entries Used to Track Prospects after a Call	
Solicitation Readiness	Rating of 1, 2, or 3 (from hot to cold)
Giving Capacity	Total giving capacity by $$ level
Ask Rating	Ask $$ level for the first solicitation
Expect Rating	Expected giving level when asked
Projected Ask Date	Enter a date for solicitation
Staff Manager	Major gift officer assigned to prospect
Volunteer	Name of volunteer who will assist
Interest Area	Program, capital, or endowment
Next Steps	Action plan with dates for each step

Building Relationships Toward Major Gifts

Most people involved in fundraising for major gifts agree that it is a relationship business. The ability of a supporter or staff member of the organization to build a personal relationship with prospects is the most crucial function of the major gift officer's activity. This personal relationship, whether it is developed over a lunch, a golf game, or years of friendship, will be the base upon which the discussion of a gift is built. Most organizations with successful major gift programs have carefully thought through the cultivation activity, or process of building relationships with donors, that results in larger gifts.

Timing of the Solicitation

Cultivation is a term used in advancement circles for the thoughtful pursuit of building a relationship between the prospective donor and the appropriate person or people connected to a nonprofit organization. In many small organizations, and in those that are new to major gift fundraising, cultivation is managed on an ad hoc basis, where it depends on the peer relationships and personal contacts of a few active board members or on personal friendships made in the community by the executive director. Although these personal connections often are important to the organization, a real major gifts program goes beyond these existing relationships to form a cultivation program.

The key problem with a casual approach to cultivation is that it limits both the size and the content of the potential major gift prospect pool. It is difficult to bring in new prospects who are unknown to current board members or the executive director if all contacts are made through personal connections with a small group of leaders. It also can be difficult for volunteer solicitors to ask for large amounts from peers and colleagues, especially if they know that they, in turn, will be asked for big gifts for their friends' favorite nonprofits.

Professional major gift staff members need to be free to establish their own connections and personal ties to potential donors beyond the limited circle of those already close to active supporters. In addition, the process of making new friends,

IN THE REAL WORLD

Making an Effective Solicitation Call

The chairman of the board of a nonprofit, the head of a large construction firm, agreed to solicit a colleague for the organization's big major gifts drive. The prospect was a peer who also owned a construction company in the same city. Both men were active in various civic causes, ranging from cultural programs to educational institutions. The prospect was rated at $100,000.

After the call, the development director met with her chairman to review the results. "Well," said the chairman, "I had him down for three other asks, including the homeless shelter, the hospital, and our school. So I just asked for them all at once, and he only gave us $25,000. There are just so many other things out there that we have to give to."

This is an example of the solicitor protecting his friend from having to give "too much" to one cause. Make sure your ask is being made effectively. If in doubt, send a team member along to keep the solicitation on target, or reassign the prospect to someone else.

bringing those friends closer to the work of the organization, and then soliciting those friends for larger gifts can result in more and larger gifts if it is professionally planned and managed.

In a more mature major gift program, cultivation is a process, one with definite objectives, steps, resources, and activities. Prospects are identified, qualified, then carried through a series of cultivation steps to provide adequate knowledge and build a relationship before a major gift is solicited. The process can vary from prospect to prospect; part of the responsibility of the major gift officer is to assess the readiness of each prospect for an ask. The cultivation process can be, and should be, personalized for each prospect's needs; again, this is the work of the major gift officer. The ultimate goal is to bring the connection between the organization and the prospect to a point where the major gift becomes a natural product of a long-term, supportive, and trusting relationship.

Without adequate cultivation, the organization puts the solicitation at risk for several problems. If the ask is made too soon in the relationship, often a smaller gift results. A solicitation made too early can result in the prospect refusing to donate or finding an excuse for putting off a decision. An early ask also can anger the donor if she feels that she is being taken for granted or being valued solely for her money and not for her involvement.

Some organizations cultivate a donor to death before making an ask. Cultivation is supposed to have an end point at which the prospect is solicited for support. Some organizations invite prospects to event after event, spend money on costly brochures, make personal visits, and yet never get to the point of asking for a gift. Donors tire of this approach also, and they lose respect for an organization that can't bring itself to ask directly for support. The major gift officer must learn to strike a happy medium between a cultivation strategy that is rushed and one that is taking too long to get to the point.

Although there are no specific rules for how long cultivation should take, many major gifts are closed between one and two years of the time that a prospective donor becomes involved with the organization. In capital campaigns, where the organization's needs and solicitation activities are very focused, this timetable sometimes can be shortened to a few months; however, in some cases, when the prospect makes a lifetime gift that involves estate planning, it can take 20 years to realize a major gift.

TIPS & TECHNIQUES

Timing of the Major Gift Solicitation Is Related to Several Factors

- The urgency of the organization's needs

- Timetable of the campaign, if one is being mounted

- The closeness of the prospect's relationship with the organization

- The judgment of the person who is closest to the prospect on the prospect's readiness

- The nature and availability of the assets that the prospect will be making the gift from

- The concurrent availability of the prospect and the members of the solicitation team

Cultivation Strategies

Because cultivation is a process, it can be broken down into a series of strategic elements that are applied to each member of the major gift prospect base. The best cultivation strategies are creative, fun to plan, and challenging to carry out. They form the core building blocks of the relationship between the prospect and the nonprofit and, as such, seek to create personal ties between people outside the organization and those already connected to the nonprofit.

Cultivation strategies build personal connections, which are essential to major gift commitments. They move prospects along a path from uninvolved to very involved with the organization. Because people of wealth tend to guard their time and involvement carefully, cultivation strategies for major gift prospects tend to move from the less personal (involvement in group activities) to more personal (face-to-face meetings). Along the way, additional activities must be planned on a personalized basis to engage the donor in the work of the organization.

Activities that introduce the prospect to the organization are referred to here as *Level I Cultivation Strategies,* because these steps provide an introduction to the nonprofit and its initiatives (see Exhibit 5.4). Level I Strategies are likely to include the prospective donor in a group activity. Cultivation strategies that involve prospects in group activities are less likely to result in initial large gifts, but they can be very effective in creating an initial tie with a prospect. Potential donors also view group events as less threatening than individual visits.

Often an invitation to a group event by print or e-mail is not enough to draw a major prospect, and a follow-up call by a board member, peer, or current donor is required to get the prospect's attention. For out-of-town events or fundraising activities, members of the host committee are asked to perform this function in order to expand the number of prospects who attend the event.

Once the prospect has been introduced to the organization, the prospect manager should move the prospect to Level II Cultivation. *Level II Cultivation Strategies* are aimed at engaging the donor in the work of the organization (see Exhibit 5.5). A prospect who respects, understands, and is involved in the work of the nonprofit will be more likely to respond positively when asked to make a financial

---

EXHIBIT 5.4

Level I Cultivation Strategies: Introduction to the Organization

- Invite the prospect to a small group dinner hosted by a major supporter.

- Invite the prospect to tour the facility with other prospects.

- Invite the prospect to screen a movie, video, or exhibit with a small group.

- Invite the prospect to the organization's annual fundraising event as the guest of a current donor or a peer.

- Invite the prospect to make a small gift in honor of a well-loved community leader.

- Invite the prospect to take part in a marketing study, feasibility study, or other activity that asks for her advice.

EXHIBIT 5.5

Level II Cultivation Strategies: Engagement with the Organization

- Ask the prospect to serve on a board or committee.

- Ask the prospect to assist with fundraising.

- Ask the prospect to provide advice in his area of expertise.

- Ask the prospect to make a small donation.

- Ask the prospect to be a volunteer in programmatic or outreach efforts.

- Ask the prospect to be the subject of an article for the newsletter.

- Ask the prospect to review a list or provide names of other prospects.

- Ask the prospect to meet with beneficiaries of the organization's services.

---

commitment. The engagement process also allows the prospective donor to create stronger personal relationships within the organization, whether those relationships are with board members, other donors, staff, or the executive leadership.

Level II Cultivation Strategies should be designed around the personal interests and background of the prospective donor. This is the work of the major gift officer who has met with the prospect, qualified her for a major gift, and learned a little about her interests and activities. The major gift officer or prospect manager should identify the best steps and strategies for involving each individual prospect in the work of the nonprofit and track those steps on a weekly or monthly basis with prospects they are responsible for.

Finally, the major gift prospect is ready for the last phase of cultivation, *Level III Cultivation Strategies* (see Exhibit 5.6). This is the most personal of all the cultivation phases. It involves the prospect on an individual, face-to-face basis with the leadership of the organization and is a direct preparation for the solicitation call. The major gift staff member is often a participant in the activities of Level III but may

RULES OF THE ROAD

Great wealth allows a person to show his true character without trying to please others. *Ninety percent of the time, this is not a good thing.*

want to bring in the assistance of the "bigger guns" at this point, including major gift committee members, campaign volunteer leaders, board members, or the organization's executive director.

The purpose of Level III activities is to inform prospects in more detail about the needs of the organization, to introduce them to the individuals who will be soliciting them, and to learn as much as possible about the prospects' philanthropic capability and intent before the ask is made. If it is possible, encourage a prospect to join a staff member or a peer on a call to another prospect whom he knows; by treating him as an "insider," the experience of working on the organization's behalf will help to convince him to make his own gift.

EXHIBIT 5.6

Level III Cultivation Strategies: Preparing for the Ask

- Have the executive director, board member, or a peer who will participate in the ask meet with the prospect, but not ask.

- Have a "money talk" between the major gifts staff member and the prospect (see the section "Talking about Money").

- Set up an intimate dinner with the prospect to make the case.

- Invite the prospect to make a speech or appear at an event, or give the prospect an award at a function.

- Give the prospect an update on the donors and gifts raised to date.

- Ask the prospect to go on a call with another supporter of the organization to help cultivate a peer or colleague.

The key to successful major gift cultivation is planning a personalized schedule of actions and steps focused on maximizing each prospect's level of interest and engagement. Cultivation is best when it proceeds according to each individual's timetable and personal preferences. Rushing to the ask, taking too long to reach the point of solicitation, or ignoring the donor for long periods of time can delay or lower the gift level. In many development offices, the tracking and planning involved with this process is called *moves management*.

Moves Management

Many major gift officers now manage between 100 and 200 prospects throughout the cultivation process, from the qualifying call to solicitation and into stewardship. How can so many prospects be personally cultivated? The rise of sophisticated development information systems has helped to sort, track, and keep records on prospects in a way that makes the process manageable.

Prospect managers are major gift staff members who are responsible for planning, tracking, and implementing the moves for each prospect assigned to them. The names of the prospect managers should be entered into the system so that all the system users know whom to talk to regarding a particular prospect. The prospect manager does not have to make every contact with each specific prospect on her list, but she must know what is planned, make the next steps happen, and organize the cultivation and solicitation of each prospect she is managing.

Most organizations try to implement a clearance policy in which prospect managers are consulted before anyone related to the nonprofit makes contact with the prospect. This minimizes multiple calls and solicitations from the same organization, which can be very embarrassing. Prospect clearance is also a means of determining which faction or interest group within an organization will get the first attempt to approach a prospect, thus providing a clearinghouse for organizations with multiple interest areas.

Prospect tracking systems allow major gifts officers the ability to enter codes and next steps for prospect actions, readiness, asks, and interest areas. Next moves, or action steps planned, can be organized by month, week, day, or geographic area. Many major gift professionals plan their call list, travel, and major cultivation events months in advance. The tools available also allow for better financial planning, since the systematic tracking of moves and solicitation dates gives the development officer a good feeling for how much money he will ask for in the next month or the next quarter.

Although advancement information systems technologies are good for planning, tracking, and making financial projections, experienced major gift officers keep their eye on the personal side of the equation also. The relationship with a donor might be managed through the computer, but it takes place in real time between real people. The human connection that develops between the staff member and the prospect is the key to making a major gift happen. Systems support is just a tool to manage a larger, more complex system of contacts—it doesn't predict outcomes or take the place of the human touch.

Building the Cultivation Continuum

Organizations that have hundreds or thousands of major gift prospects to cultivate and ask have developed ongoing programs for cultivation and solicitation to create a more efficient pattern of activity with donors. Looking at cultivation in a systematic way allows nonprofits to stay focused on producing activity that results in real gifts. For campaigns with a specific timetable, or major gift programs that involve national travel and outreach, creating a cultivation continuum is a practical way to build ties, develop relationships, and still hold to the bottom line.

The cultivation continuum is a system for recognizing and creating a pattern of activity that results in moving a prospect from the qualifying call through the cultivation process to a successful solicitation. As noted, the process tends to move the prospect through three stages of cultivation, from introduction to the organization, through engagement, to preparation for the solicitation. With the cultivation continuum, the organization provides a specific path for each stage of the cultivation process, centered on the production of events and opportunities for engagement that meet the needs of donors at each point in the process. These activities can be repeated in different cities around the country, or they can be repeated on an annual basis to bring new prospects into the continuum.

Sample Cultivation Continuum
Used by an Art Museum

Level I: Introduction

The advancement director identified 150 prospects capable of making a gift of $10,000 or more to the museum's new major gifts initiative. She and the director then found several current supporters who agreed to host small group dinners in their homes on behalf of the museum. The elegant dinners, paid for by the host, included a brief presentation by the museum's director, a statement of support from the host, and a preview of items from an upcoming exhibit.

Level II: Engagement

After the dinners, each prospective donor was visited by an advancement staff member. The call served to determine interest, capability, and readiness to make a gift. It also allowed the development officer to identify a plan for involvement in the museum that matched the prospect's interests.

In addition, each prospect was asked to join the leadership annual donor group, the Museum Partners, with an annual gift of $1,000. Joining the Museum Partners created additional opportunities for engagement, because the membership benefits included attending an annual event, invitations to exhibition openings, and a monthly newsletter.

Level III: Preparation for the Solicitation

Each of the prospects was then assigned to a volunteer. Volunteers included the chairman of the board, the chair of the board development committee, and the members of the major gifts committee. Each volunteer took five prospects. The volunteers invited their prospects to meet for lunch in the museum garden café, where they explained the needs further and toured the museum. No ask was made.

Solicitation

Solicitation teams included a volunteer, a staff member, and a board member or the museum director, when appropriate. Over 50% of the prospects, or 75 donors, ultimately committed to a gift of $10,000 or more. Several made six- and seven-figure gifts.

Talking About Money

It may sound peculiar, because fundraising is all about money, but some fundraisers are uncomfortable bringing up the subject of money. Perhaps this is a function of old-school social taboos, in which talking about money was viewed as crass, impolite, or bragging. Perhaps the fundraiser's emphasis on building personal relationships interferes with his interest in getting a gift from the donor, making it awkward to bring up the subject. Sometimes the donor is the one who puts off financial discussions as a way of protecting herself against a solicitation that she knows will cost her money. Whatever the case, major gift programs that succeed do focus on the money. The development world is awash in stories of donors who are cultivated to death but never asked. The question of when to bring up money, and how to do so, has many different possible answers.

Qualifying Calls: To Ask or Not to Ask?

Getting money is not the main focus of the qualifying call. Whether to ask for a gift the first time a staff member meets with a prospect depends on the fundraiser's comfort level and the circumstances of the call (see Exhibit 5.7). An ask on a first visit can seem pushy to donors, who may be expecting an informational meeting, not a solicitation, in their first exposure to the organization. There is a case to be made, however, for making a small ask—often for an annual fund gift—during the initial qualifying call.

Many experienced major gift officers view asking for a small gift at the first meeting as an appropriate, even a preferred, way to begin the cultivation process

---

EXHIBIT 5.7

Pros and Cons of Asking for a Gift on the First Meeting with a Donor

Pros

- Early asks can be used as cultivation steps toward a larger gift.
- It involves the donor in the work of the organization.
- It gives the organization a good reason to stay in touch.
- It puts money on the table from the beginning—more honest.
- It brings in money for the annual fund.

Cons

- The donor can see the ask as too pushy or too soon.
- The donor doesn't know the organization very well yet.
- The donor can use an early ask to "lowball" his gift size.
- It allows the donor to get "off the hook" by saying he already gave.

---

toward a larger gift. If the prospect is even mildly interested in the organization, an initial gift can be a way for him to "buy into" the organization, to show support, and to encourage additional contact. Most wealthy prospects will not be surprised at being asked for money—they are already experienced donors to a variety of organizations. They know why a development officer from a nonprofit has set up a visit with them. For many major gift officers, there is really no reason to play a cat-and-mouse game with a prospective donor. Everyone involved knows that money is at least part of the equation.

The first gift, often a small one, can be used as a preliminary step for bringing a potentially large donor on board. Making a gift, no matter what the size, involves the donor in the work of the organization and serves as a means for putting him on the mailing list, maintaining communication, and making follow-up visits. Making an ask on the initial visit actually can create a better atmosphere for the discussion of a major gift later, because the prospect understands from the beginning that the organization needs his financial support. As mentioned, usually with major gift prospects, the initial ask is made at the leadership level for the annual fund.

There are also good reasons *not* to ask at the first meeting. Some donors, particularly older, more conservative people with roots in the Depression era, find a focus on money too early in the relationship to be offensive. They may want to be wooed, to learn more, or to become more involved in the work of the organization. The development officer will have to use judgment in such cases. At times, in order to set the appointment with the prospect, the staff member may have had to promise that "no solicitation would be made." This can be useful to get in the door, but it is not a good long-term strategy to use with a potential major gift donor. At some point, the discussion must turn to money, and whether it is on the first call or the tenth, it is more honest to make the organization's interests clear from the start.

Some fundraisers feel that asking at the first meeting allows a wealthy prospect to "lowball" a potential major gift, by writing a small check to get rid of the solicitor. The strategy to use here is to ask for a leadership level annual fund gift, not a gift that could be construed by the donor as a small major gift or a gift to the campaign. Annual gifts, by definition, involve the donor in supporting the operational budget of the organization and thus offer the opportunity for future engagement in the cultivation process; yet donors who make major gifts at the low end of the gift chart may believe they have already met the needs of the organization. There is a subtle, but not too complex, psychology at work here. The major gift officer wants to ask for a gift that will keep the door open with the donor; the donor may be trying to make a gift that will close the door to a future ask.

The Money Talk

In advancement programs where major gift work has become more mature, staff members look for an opportunity to have a "money talk" with the major gift prospect before a formal solicitation call is made. The purpose of the money talk is to have the major gifts staff member conduct reconnaissance work before sending in the heavyweight solicitation team. The efficient organization does not want to waste the time of its board members, campaign leaders, or CEO. If the prospect still has major questions about the organization, is not capable of making a major gift at this time, or has other issues that need to be resolved before making a gift, it is far better to learn about these problems ahead of the ask than to embarrass both the donor and a roomful of solicitors.

Having the money talk is more than conducting an early assessment of the prospect's readiness for the solicitation team. In an ideal world, the major gift officer has already developed a good, open relationship with the prospect as part of the cultivation process. Talk about a major gift should flow naturally from the ongoing dialogue between the development staff member and the donor about the needs and progress of the organization.

When turning the discussion to money, the staff member must be candid and considerate of the donor's needs and desires. He should strive to preserve the best elements of the relationship with the donor while still representing the interests and needs of the nonprofit. In the best of donor/staff relationships, the donor feels free to tell the major gift officer how she wants to be solicited.

The use of the major gift staff member to start the conversation about a major gift brings with it several advantages:

- The donor may be more willing to ask questions in private, with a staff member, than in front of the organization's director or trustees.

- The donor may be more willing to share information about the gift he wants to make in a private conversation.

- The donor is often more open with a staff member about his financial issues than he would be in front of peers or colleagues.

- The donor can use the conversation with a staff member to have input into how the solicitation will be handled.

Perhaps the major disadvantage in using the major gift staff member to initiate such a conversation comes when donors are trying to put off the ask. They can be more abrupt with the staff member and simply say they are not going to make a gift. Because the leverage inherent in having peers and colleagues in on the solicitation call is missing, donors can move to a refusal more quickly. In most cases, however, the goal of the staff member's conversation—to prepare both the solicitation team and the donor for the solicitation call—is still met, although unfortunately the answer turns out to be no.

The staff member can use one of several techniques to learn more about the donor's giving preferences. The first option is simply to openly discuss the pending call with the donor. The staff member can say that she has heard a call is in the works, she can reference the urgent nature of a pressing need, or she can suggest that the campaign timetable is pressing. This gives her an opening to ask the donor who should come on the call, how it should be set up, and who should be present. Learning personal preferences, such as whether the spouse should be present in the ask, can make the difference between a large gift and no gift.

Another possibility is to use one of several fundraising tools as a starting point for the discussion (see Exhibit 5.8). Some major gift officers prefer to share a gift table, a chart that shows the potential giving levels and numbers of donors in desired gift ranges, with the donor and ask, "Where do you see yourself on this chart?" Others will prepare a list of naming options in the ranges above and down to the prospective donor's rated giving level, asking him to review the options presented. Presenting naming options allows the staff member to discuss recognition issues that could provide an incentive for the donor to make a larger gift. Showing the prospect a list of current major donors with their gift level provides the opportunity for a similar exchange and puts the pending solicitation in both a social and financial context for the prospect.

Timing also can be addressed with the donor ahead of the ask. The donor might reveal, for instance, that he is about to sell his company and needs to put off a meeting

---

EXHIBIT 5.8

Tools to Use to Talk about Money

1. Gift table

2. List of recognition opportunities with prices

3. Architectural drawings or blueprints (for a capital project)

4. List of major gifts already made with donor names

TIPS & TECHNIQUES

Desired Outcomes: Having a Pre-Solicitation Discussion with the Prospect

- Learn who the prospect wants to be solicited by
- Find out who else should be present during the call (i.e., spouse, children, partner)
- Determine what the prospect expects the ask amount to be and what he is willing to give
- Explore what recognition, if any, he desires
- Discuss what financial resources will be used to make the gift

for six months; or, if the donor is engaged in estate planning, his plans could affect the timing, the vehicle, and the amount of the gift. Some donors will ask that the presentation be made in front of members of the family foundation board. The point is that you don't know until you ask what assumptions are being made, what the donor's expectations are, and what amount he is already considering for his gift.

Summary

The first step toward opening the door to a major gift prospect is the qualifying call. From there, providing attentive, creative, and personal cultivation is the key to building relationships with potential major donors. Building relationships with donors has come a long way in the era of development information systems. Efficient and effective major gift program directors think about ways to systematize their cultivation efforts; they move prospects along a continuum of action steps, directed by an overall plan that introduces and engages donors in the work of the organization, then prepares them for a successful solicitation call.

In the face of this systematic activity, creating an open and trusting relationship between the major gift officer and the prospect is increasingly important. The development officer should manage and plan the prospect's interaction with the organization. She should also be able to ask for gifts, talk about money, and learn about the donor's preferences with the ease that comes from experience and good interpersonal skills. Her involvement, from the qualifying call through cultivation and solicitation to stewardship, is the crucial element that will provide a smooth relationship between the major gift donor and the nonprofit institution.

CHAPTER 6

Soliciting Major Gifts

After reading this chapter you will be able to:

- Prepare for the ask
- Make a successful solicitation call
- Close the gift

Preparing for the Ask

As with most tasks in life, preparation in major gift work is half the battle. Most organizations get only one shot at soliciting a major potential donor. They must prepare carefully, pooling all their knowledge, research, and experience with the individual to formulate a strategy that augers well for success. This is not the time to shoot from the hip or to play it by ear.

The process of major gift prospect cultivation and solicitation is a fluid one that requires flexibility from all the participants. A number of analogies come to mind that could be used to describe the unique give-and-take, ebb and flow, of this singular relationship. Some development officers think of the process as a dance, a graceful series of movements back and forth with the prospect, always leading in the ultimate direction of the gift. Others subscribe to the more masculine imagery of the battle and wartime activity: The organization's needs are organized into a campaign, which requires well-trained troops who target prospects for a gift.

Taking the analogies one step further, the fundraiser could be viewed as a diplomat, creating a special tie or a bridge between opposing forces, using the tools of good communication and personal relationships. Some of the best solicitors enjoy approaching fundraising as if it were a game; they operate as if they were moving pieces on a chess board, constantly planning strategy three or four moves ahead of where the action is taking place. Although winning is important, always remember that the solution that provides a winning hand for both sides of the equation is the ultimate goal.

Whether viewed as a game, a dance, a war tactic, or the shuffle of diplomacy, the solicitation process is one that should be planned carefully. Most solicitations in a staff-driven program are directed by the prospect manager, who must strategize carefully to maximize the donor's potential giving.

Select the Team

Either the prospect manager or the person with the nonprofit who is connected most closely to the prospect should identify the team members who will make the solicitation call. It is possible, of course, to ask for money using only one solicitor. Often the president of a university or the chairman of the board of a nonprofit will have the experience, clout, and comfort level to ask a major donor for a large gift one-on-one. If the solicitor is experienced and the relationship with the donor is a good one, this can be a successful model; however, it gives the solicitor little room to negotiate, and it may limit the reach of the organization if only one leader conducts most of the solicitations.

Many major gift officers also ask for money successfully, alone or with other volunteers or staff members accompanying them. In general, the bigger the ask, the higher the level of volunteer or staff member who should be included. In larger organizations and in much campaign work, major gift officers become adept at asking for gifts of $10,000 to $250,000 or so by themselves but bring in support for gifts of $500,000 or more. Even in multimillion-dollar asks, the development professional can play a key role as a member of the team, making sure that the ask is made and answering questions the prospect may pose about the gift.

IN THE REAL WORLD

The Crowded Room

A solicitation call was arranged with a new member of the board of a non-profit during a capital campaign. The board member was a well-known philanthropist and the ask level was set high—at $2 million. It was an important leadership gift for the campaign, and the meeting was set to include the chairman of the board, the chair of the campaign, and the executive director.

On the day of the meeting, there was some confusion about where it would take place. The big conference room had a group in it that couldn't be moved. The director's office hadn't been cleaned up after some water damage. Then the chairman of the development committee arrived and thought *he* was supposed to be part of the solicitation team too. Nobody would agree to defer to anyone else, so they all decided to stay.

The group squeezed around a small table in the advancement director's office. When they emerged 20 minutes later, they were glum. The donor had promised $500,000, one-quarter of the amount they had hoped for.

The advancement director called the donor the next day to ask what had happened. "Well, I felt squeezed in there, like they were all pushing me up against the wall," responded the donor. "I didn't feel comfortable with all four of them breathing down my neck, so I gave them the first number I could come up with just to get out of there."

Who should make up the solicitation team? This is a judgment call based on the organization's knowledge and experience with the prospect. Most successful solicitors prefer to bring two to three people on a call, as larger groups tend to obscure the mission and overwhelm the prospect. An exception might be made for a scheduled meeting with a foundation board or a corporate giving committee, where a more formal presentation can be structured. In such a case, bringing along four or five individuals to help present the organization's needs might be appropriate, but only if each person has a specific, identified role to play (see Exhibit 6.1).

The choice of which people to bring along for a call on an individual major gift prospect is crucial. Most organizations include the person who knows the prospect the best. This may be a major gift officer, the chief executive officer, a program

---

EXHIBIT 6.1

Prepare the Solicitation Team for the Call

The solicitation team should have access to:

- The prospect's connection to the organization

- The prospect's giving history with the organization

- Biographical information, including spouse's name, names of children, name and title of business, and home location

- Summary of research results on the prospect

- Ask amount and purpose of the ask

- Relevant personal information (i.e., recent divorce, health issues, pending sale of company, etc.)

---

officer, or a volunteer. They also bring along someone who can speak to the project at hand, because making the case for why the organization needs the money is one objective of the meeting. Finally, the group must include someone who is willing to ask. Usually this is an executive or staff member with the nonprofit, but some volunteers are excellent solicitors and can be very persuasive with donors.

The use of volunteers on a solicitation call is governed by the organization's access to experienced volunteers and the volunteer's ties to the prospect. The volunteer, in order to be effective, should already have pledged her own gift. Sometimes this means that a particular call on a prospect has to be preceded by the solicitation of the volunteer who will be needed to make that call. This is worth the time and effort! A volunteer who can say that she is only asking the prospect to do what she herself has already done makes the best possible case and is hard to turn down.

Some volunteers are more experienced in fundraising than others. If a volunteer refuses to ask, or expresses discomfort at asking, consider having that person make the case as part of the team, then turn the ask portion of the call over to a professional staff member. Also consider using volunteers to set up the appointment or follow-up after the meeting. Ideally, the best volunteer to use on a solicitation call

TIPS & TECHNIQUES

Four Basic Rules of Major Gift Solicitations

1. The most important element of the call is who is included on the team.

2. A volunteer asking for money should already have made a gift of his own.

3. Prepare all the team members for the call and assign roles.

4. A solicitation where no money is asked for is not a successful call.

is a peer or colleague of the prospect, someone he knows and respects, who has already made her own commitment to the project at hand. If no such person is available, use someone whose name or title will impress the potential donor: Campaign chairs, board chairs, and community leaders are all appropriate choices, even when they aren't personally known to the prospect.

Make the Appointment

Unlike a qualifying call, the purpose of the solicitation appointment is to ask the prospect for money. Although the appointment setter doesn't literally have to spell this out, it is best to answer the donor's questions about the appointment directly. The caller can say that the appointment concerns a "potential giving opportunity" or that the callers want to "discuss the campaign for such and such a need." If the staff member has had an opportunity to hold the "money talk" with the prospect, as described in Chapter 5, the donor will know exactly what to expect. Most wealthy prospects are very familiar with the solicitation process. If there are repeated delays in setting the appointment or the donor point-blank refuses to accept the meeting, that in itself is a hint that more cultivation is needed.

Where should the solicitation meeting take place? Often the best place is one that the donor chooses. Making sure that the donor is comfortable is important, and that can mean seeing him on his own ground. Although some solicitors love asking for money at meals, often restaurants and coffee shops don't afford the level of privacy that such a discussion demands. Noise, interruptions, pushy waiters, and long waits for tables are all a turn-off for a meeting that needs to go smoothly. Private rooms can work but may seem too stuffy. Consider meeting with the prospect at his home, his office, his boardroom, his club, or another place of his choosing that is private and comfortable. For out-of-town prospects, an attempt should be made to travel to the prospect's home city for a sizable solicitation.

When making the appointment call, always state clearly who will be going along to represent the nonprofit. If the prospect is unfamiliar with the names, state what role each person plays with the nonprofit, such as: *Bob is the co-chair of our campaign,* or *Sarah is the director of program outreach.* Always send a short note to confirm the date, place, and time of the meeting, and call the prospect a day ahead to reconfirm. Most individuals of wealth lead very busy lives, have complicated schedules, and will appreciate the professionalism of the organization at this juncture.

Assign Roles

A successful solicitation is more than a group pressure tactic. The major gift solicitation has a specific series of five components, or steps, starting with introducing the need and explaining why the gift is needed (Exhibit 6.2). The ask ensues, followed by a period of give-and-take that usually includes listening to the response, answering questions, and countering objections. Finally, in what some view as the most difficult portion of the call, a team member moves to close the gift. Although closure of the gift often takes place at a later date, the terms under which the meeting is ended are especially significant.

The solicitation team should discuss each of these elements in advance, with roles assigned to each member of the team. Plan to practice ahead of time through a

 RULES OF THE ROAD

If you're calling on the head of Microsoft, don't carry an Apple laptop computer.

EXHIBIT 6.2

5 Elements of the Successful Solicitation Call

1. Opening Moves	5 to 10 minutes
2. Making the Case	10 to 15 minutes
3. Making the Ask	5 to 10 minutes
4. Active Listening	5 to 20 minutes
5. Closing the Ask	5 minutes
Total Call Time:	**30 minutes to 1 hour**

conference call or a presolicitation meeting. Running through the plan ahead of time is helpful, especially if the team includes members who haven't worked together before or inexperienced volunteers. The staff can write out scripts or outlines and provide them to team members to help each one remember key points.

Taking the time to prepare for a call, such as assigning roles, preparing scripts, and practicing lines, can seem like an unnecessary burden to the experienced solicitor. For those who don't do this work everyday, however, the process of preparing for the ask provides a helpful sense of security and order in an activity that can make some people very anxious. When staff members use the preparation time to train, focus, and ready the team, everyone involved is reassured that the best possible approach is being made to the prospect, whatever the outcome may be. Good preparation helps to counter recriminations later.

Development professionals estimate that between three and four prospects are needed for every gift closed. Many major gift professionals beat this ratio, because they work hard to assess the donor's level of interest and commitment before the ask is made. In any case, not every solicitation will be successful, and the outcome may have very little to do with the skills of the team or the importance of the need. Solicitations fail for an untold number of reasons, ranging from changing financial circumstances to differing priorities regarding philanthropic support. It is important to remind volunteers and other team members of this so that, if the call does not result in a gift, they don't take the rejection personally.

Steps to Making a Successful Solicitation

There are five identifiable steps to the solicitation call. Each step needs to be planned and assigned to a team member as part of the major gift solicitation strategy. These steps range from the opening moves, which can be a simple introduction of the team members present, to the close, which often determines when and how the deal will be clinched. The entire call should take anywhere from 30 minutes to an hour. Anything shorter usually means that steps were skipped, and longer calls often cause the team to wear out its welcome.

1. Opening Moves: 5 to 10 Minutes

The goal of the opening moves in the call is to make the prospect feel comfortable with the solicitation team. One team member should take charge at the very beginning of the meeting and lead the conversation. This role can be assigned to a peer or colleague of the donor.

Allow all members of the team to introduce themselves and explain their role within the organization clearly. Team members should strive to set a familiar tone, to put everyone at ease, and to bring the group to the point of readiness for the business portion of the meeting.

Opening conversational gambits can be off the subject for a moment or two; this is the time to comment on the weather, discuss the donor's recent vacation, or ask after a family member's health. No more than 5 to 10 minutes should be spent on the opening moves in order to leave plenty of time for the key points in the meeting.

The team member in charge should plan a transition point, smoothly moving the conversation to the business at hand by referring to "the reason we are all here," and turning to the person who will be making the case, nodding to her to go ahead. Staying in the opening moves part of the visit for too long can be awkward; the team leader should make sure that momentum is building and the conversation doesn't drag before making this transition.

2. Making the Case: 10 to 15 Minutes

Making the case is the point in the meeting where passion should be displayed. The team member assigned to make the case must be intimately involved with and informed about the organization in order to make this portion of the call effective. Real passion can be very moving and very persuasive. The person who makes the case can be a committed volunteer, a program director, a recipient of the organization's services, or a staff member, as long as his commitment is palpable and real.

The person who makes the case must explain clearly what the need is, why it is there, and what the donor can do to remedy it by making this gift. If supportive materials are going to be used, this is the portion of the meeting in which to display them.

Supportive materials can take many forms. Consider using:

- A short video

- A PowerPoint presentation

- A brochure

- Photographs in a notebook

- Renderings and architectural plans (for capital campaigns)

Many solicitors talk too long at this point. Making the case should take from 10 to 15 minutes. By this stage, the prospect should have been cultivated enough so that she is familiar with the organization, its mission, its goals, and its general needs. Making the case at this point should focus on the specifics: how her gift will meet a special need, what opportunities meeting this need will create for the organization, how the resulting services will be provided, and what people it will serve.

Use good communications techniques while presenting the case to the prospect. Don't talk *at* her; instead, include her in the conversation by pausing to see that she is following, encouraging her to ask questions, and directing questions back to her. Try to bring the prospect into the conversation as a participant, not just a listener. Be careful about using humor and off-color stories (which can backfire), and be sure that any anecdotes told are short and make a relevant point.

At the end of the case presentation, pause and ask the prospect if she has questions about anything that has been said.

127

3. Making the Ask: 5 to 10 Minutes

The solicitation portion of the meeting can be made more dynamic if a different team member takes over. The team member who makes the case should provide an appropriate segue in the conversation, for example, by nodding to the solicitor and introducing him by saying: "Now John here wants to talk to you about how you can help us with this."

The solicitor may choose to "frame the ask" at this point, setting the context for the gift by introducing either a gift chart or a list of current donors (see "Tips & Techniques" on page 133). Doing so brings additional peer pressure to bear on the donor and introduces the gift levels, or range of levels, where the ask will reside. Once the solicitor has set the context for the gift, he moves immediately into the ask (see Exhibit 6.3).

The solicitation should include a dollar amount, a purpose, and the recognition that is awarded to a gift at that level. These elements should be incorporated into one phrase or a short summary statement that encompasses the entire solicitation in a pithy, focused manner. Don't drag it out, and don't be obtuse or obscure; this is a moment for clarity (see Exhibit 6.4).

All major gift officers are well trained in what happens after the ask is made: The solicitation team remains quiet and waits for the donor to respond. This self-imposed silence can seem painfully long and awkward as the seconds tick by, but don't break

---

EXHIBIT 6.3

Examples of How to Ask for Major Gifts

- We would like to ask you to make a gift of $2 million to name the new wing of the museum. A gift of this size would allow you to name the wing.

- Would you give the first $100,000 to underwrite our new program? You will be identified as the sponsor when we start the program next spring.

- Please help us by contributing $10,000 toward the new literacy program. Your name would be listed on the brass plaque in the lobby at the patron's level.

EXHIBIT 6.4

A Solicitation Should
Include Three Elements

- A specific ask amount (i.e., $10,000, $2 million)

- A specific purpose for the gift (i.e., for the endowed chair in engineering or for the capital campaign to build the new wing of the museum)

- A specific recognition or benefit that goes along with the gift (i.e., your name will be on the chair, or you will be listed on our donor wall in front of the auditorium)

---

it! Advancement insiders say that after the ask, he who speaks first loses. If by that they mean that the donor loses when he makes a gift, they are misstating the case. However, the point is that the donor should be allowed time to think, react, and respond before the team jumps in.

Common problems that occur at this point in the call include:

- Solicitations that are not specific enough

- Solicitations that don't include an ask amount

- Solicitations that don't present a giving option

- Solicitations that use language that makes the gift too tentative

- Solicitations that sound apologetic

These frequently encountered problems can be practiced and dealt with in advance through training and role-playing. Above all, don't apologize for asking for money! Be bold, have confidence in what you are doing, and your confidence will help to convince the donor.

4. Active Listening: 5 to 20 Minutes

After the ask is made, the job of the solicitation team is to listen carefully, respond, and deal with objections as they are rendered. It is called active listening because the team has to move conceptually with the donor, following his line of thought and reacting to his concerns. It is unlikely that the donor will agree immediately to the amount and purpose as posed in the solicitation. It is more common to have the donor respond with questions, make excuses for delays, make a counter offer, or air grievances. The team needs to evaluate the donor's responses seriously and give them due attention.

There are exceptions to every rule. Occasionally a situation will require some alteration from the standard solicitation just outlined. Some donors want to select the purpose of their gift from a list of options; team members can accommodate by carrying along a list of needs and naming opportunities. Some donors will want to pin down the amount before getting to the purpose. Others will try to negotiate more recognition or up the ante by offering a smaller gift for the same recognition. This give-and-take becomes part of the donor's response and requires active listening from the team.

After the ask portion of the call, the donor's questions can run the gamut from simple to complex:

- Sophisticated: *Will any of my gift be spent on overhead, or will it all go to capital?*

- Intrusive: *Can I hire the professor who will hold this endowed chair?*

- Uninformed: *What did you say the goal was?*

- Financial planning: *Can I pledge it over five years?*

- Request for further consideration: *Can I talk to my wife about this?*

The fact that the donor asks questions is a good sign, because having questions shows interest and engagement with the institution. Questions must be answered openly and honestly. If you don't know the answer, don't make it up! Offer to find out the answer and get back to the donor as soon as possible.

Delaying tactics are common responses to a major gift solicitation. Sometimes donors will not explain why they need to hold off, but they will proffer excuses or indicate that they need more time to reach a decision. It is not always clear whether donors mean the excuse literally, because they really do need more time to consider

Investing in Relationships

The hospital had experienced numerous ups and downs in its advancement budget over the years, requiring the staff to suffer through a series of layoffs. It seemed the next to go would be Bob, a senior major gift staff member who had been with the program for many years. As time went on, he made fewer calls, traveled less, and generally was viewed as unproductive.

The vice president, however, refused to let Bob go, mostly because he remained very close to one of the hospital's wealthiest donors, an elderly widow. For years he had been driving her to doctor's appointments, escorting her to hospital functions, and squiring her around town. When she eventually passed away, it turned out she had made a $50 million bequest to the hospital, much more than they ever dreamed she would do.

Bob, the unproductive staff member, was paid the equivalent of $70,000 a year for 20 years—not a bad investment to produce a gift of $50 million!

the gift, or whether they are just being polite and don't want to say no. If no other information is available, it is best to take the reason proffered at face value and get donors to agree on a date for the next contact.

5. Closing the Gift: 5 Minutes

Closing a gift is an art, not a science. The team member assigned to close the gift must take into account all of the give-and-take exchanged in the meeting up to this point. Like a dancer, he must have an instinct for when to lead and when to back off. Like a diplomat, he must differentiate between concerns that are real issues and those that are merely thrown up as excuses. Like a general, he can help to strong-arm the conversation by moving the discussion back to the gift. And, like a chess player, he must plan several moves ahead to assess and meet the donor's needs and desires.

The key to closing the gift is for the donor and the solicitation team to agree on a next step and the time frame for that next step before leaving the meeting. The next step should be developed as a response to the reactions or concerns that the donor expressed during the active listening period. The closer should outline—out loud, for all to agree with—a brief plan to meet the objections, delays, questions, and negotiating points that the donor has brought up during the meeting. The closing, therefore, is always personalized to the needs of the prospective donor and the situation at hand.

Closing the meeting can be a simple matter, such as agreeing to drawing up a pledge letter, or complex, such as agreeing to look into allegations of financial impropriety. The prospective donor must leave the meeting feeling that his concerns have been heard and that they will be addressed adequately. It is useful at the end of the meeting for the closer to repeat the donor's main issues, explain how they will

IN THE REAL WORLD

When the CEO Won't Ask

The long-serving director of a major nonprofit was well loved by everyone in the community, including his donors, his board, and his staff. The advancement director, however, was at his wits' end. He just could not get the director to capitalize on his wonderful relationships and ask the donors for money. The advancement staff could list many occasions where they felt that "money had been left on the table" through the director's passive approach to fundraising. What could they do?

After attending a seminar and talking to some peers, the advancement director came up with a plan. He accepted the director's limitations and decided to work on a two-stage solicitation process. The director would cultivate and bring prospects into the fold; then another solicitor would follow up, taking advantage of the strong relationships developed by the director to ask for money.

It worked like a charm. Three solicitors were selected and trained: the assistant director, an experienced board member, and the advancement director himself took on a group of prospects. Their fundraising tag-team approach doubled the major gifts to the organization within 12 months.

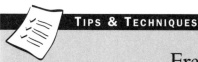

Framing the Ask

Framing the ask is a technique that gives donors a context for the level and purpose of their gifts. There are several ways to accomplish this technique:

- The solicitor can use a gift chart, showing donors the levels near and above the proposed gift, and explain how important it is to meet the higher levels to make the project work.

- The solicitor can bring out a list of current donors who have made gifts near and above the level the donor is being asked for. This is especially helpful if the donor recognizes some of the names on the list.

- The solicitor can mention his own gift level, saying, for example: "I've already made my gift for a classroom in the new building, and I'd like you to think about doing the same."

be resolved, and set forward a timetable for the resolution. Doing this ensures that all parties have come to a similar understanding in the meeting, even if no final decision on the gift has been reached.

Closing the gift can take place at the meeting, a few days after the meeting, or months later. In general, the longer it takes from the time of the meeting to close the gift, the less the chances of receiving the gift, so there is some need for speed in the follow-up timetable. As the donor moves further from the sense of passionate commitment and urgency communicated during the solicitation call, it becomes more difficult to keep her focused on the organization's needs. Other interests intervene, and the routine of daily life takes its toll on her attention span.

An important exception to this rule of thumb is the donor who is preparing to make a planned gift, since estate planning requires both a significant amount of time and the involvement of financial planning experts. Planned giving and its role in major gift giving is discussed in more detail in Chapter 8.

TIPS & TECHNIQUES

Examples of Weak Asking Techniques

- I know it's a lot to ask, and I appreciate the fact that your profits are down, but could you give us $25,000? (Too negative. Don't give the donor excuses.)

- Whatever you could give would be much appreciated. (Too vague. Always ask for a specific amount.)

- Would you like to do that gift over 5 years or 10 years? (Don't let the donor off the hook. The nonprofit needs the cash flow.)

Common Issues in Negotiating and Closing Gifts

1. "The Gift Level Is Too High"

Offer to have him spread out the gift over five years as part of a pledge agreement. Note that no timetable for the gift has been proposed in the solicitation itself. Pledges, timing, and the duration of the payout period are points that should be brought up after the ask has been made. These issues should become part of the response to the ask and often may require some negotiation; the solicitation team should not make assumptions about the donor's ability to pay the full amount. Some donors pull out their checkbook and write a check for the full amount of the gift on the day they agree to it. Others need 10 years to pay it off in small segments. Don't make assumptions about pledge timing that could delay cash flow to your organization.

2. "I Was Unhappy with the Way My Name Appeared in the Donor Honor Roll Last Year"

Respond to complaints by giving the donor a sympathetic hearing and providing due process in the follow-up while reinforcing the need to finalize the discussion about the gift. At times the donor will air grievances with the organization as a way of putting off committing to the gift. This kind of response can be viewed as either a delaying tactic or in some cases a negotiating point. Perhaps the donor is just being difficult or wants to test the organization. A donor can force the nonprofit to spend a lot of time jumping through hoops trying to answer a grievance or explaining some perceived injustice. Each organization will have to weigh the costs and benefits of committing major staff time to fixing complaints.

The solicitation team should take the donor's concerns seriously, try to address them, return with an answer, and then ask for the gift again. A good fundraiser views a complaint as an invitation to fix something, not a door closed in the face. Negative engagement is still engagement, annoying though it may be!

3. "I Need to Consult with My Wife before Making a Decision"

Accept the need for consultation gracefully, offer to provide another meeting with the spouse, and agree on the timing of the next contact. Many donors use this as a tactic to put off making a decision right away. It can either be a legitimate need or an excuse. The organization might plan to deal with this issue up front by including the spouse in the call; however, this should be addressed when the appointment is made. Some delays actually may improve the chances for receiving a gift: "I need to check with my accountant," for instance, can be a good sign, especially for year-end giving. Be sure that a team member follows up with the donor after the promised interval.

4. "I'm Interested in Naming the New Wing, but I Can Give Only $1 Million, Not $2 Million"

Don't agree to do anything for one donor that you wouldn't agree to for others. Counter-offers and negotiations about naming opportunities can cause difficulty, especially if the donor expects more recognition or "bang for the buck" than what is being offered. Certain donors seem to enjoy the art of negotiating and get a charge out of asking for a special deal from the organization. If you are ready to drop all the prices, go ahead, but special deals never stay secret. Dropping the price of a naming opportunity will affect the gift levels your organization can achieve from all your other donors.

Other options for response include: asking the donor to pledge the money over a longer period of time, introducing the idea of funding the gift through a lead trust,

RULES OF THE ROAD

A volunteer is someone who can drive you crazy faster than your boss can but who doesn't pay you to put up with it.

asking him to get another $1 million from a friend and name the project for both of them, or just refuse and offer him another lower-priced naming opportunity.

5. "I'm Involved in Estate Planning Right Now"

This situation provides an opening to move the gift discussion to planned giving options. Offer to send him some information, ask him whether you can talk with his financial advisor, or offer a specific planned gift tool (e.g., a trust) that might meet his goals for the gift currently under discussion.

Additional hints that indicate the time is right for a planned giving discussion include: statements about imminent retirement, explanations about the need to take care of a spouse or child, or a pending change of financial status, such as the sale of a family company.

The use of planned gifts in major gift giving is discussed in more detail in Chapter 8. At least one member of the solicitation team should be familiar with the major vehicles in planned gifts. The point is not to negotiate every detail of the gift at this meeting but to know enough to bring up the concept, discuss the appropriate vehicle, and open the door to further discussions with the donor or his financial advisors.

Summary

Major gift solicitations require careful advance planning to deliver the best results. Strategic thinking is required to determine the best team to make the call, who should make the case, and who should close the gift. It is useful to practice or write out scripts and outlines for each participant to ensure that the call goes smoothly. Give call participants access to a summary of the most recent research information that the organization has gathered on the prospect in order to bring them up to date on the prospect's current personal and financial circumstances.

TIPS & TECHNIQUES

Examples of Closing Agreements

- We agree to accept a pledge over five years. We'll draw up a pledge letter and send it to you for your review tomorrow.

- I understand your concerns about that PR debacle last year. We will look into it and get back to you in the next week. Can I call you to follow up on our discussion at that time?

- We would be happy to talk with your wife about the gift. When do you think would be a good time to meet with both of you?

- We would like to invite you to visit our facilities to see the program for yourself. Do you think you could come next week?

- We'd like to prepare a proposal for you that explores the alternatives we have discussed. Is next week soon enough?

- We would really like to wrap the campaign up before next June. Do you think we could meet with you again in three months?

There are five distinct elements to a solicitation call: (1) opening comments, (2) making the case, (3) making the ask, (4) listening and overcoming objections, and (5) closing the gift. Each of these elements has its own timing and strategic importance in keeping the call momentum going. Participants should agree who will take charge of each element and practice, or role-play, before the call is made.

Overcoming objections raised by the donor and closing the gift can be the most demanding activities in major gift fundraising. The closer must find a way to reach an agreement with the donor on how his objections or concerns will be treated, what the next contact with the organization will be, and set the timetable for that contact. The donor must leave the meeting feeling that his concerns have been taken seriously, that he has been listened to with respect, and that the organization has benefited from his involvement. The team participants should leave the meeting feeling that they were properly prepared, that they handled the donor's issues appropriately, and that they know what next steps they need to take to keep the gift moving toward closure.

CHAPTER 7

Motivating Donors: Recognition and Stewardship

After reading this chapter you will be able to:

- Provide appropriate donor recognition
- Prepare and price naming opportunities
- Use good stewardship to build towards the next gift

Motivating Donors through Recognition

Motivating donors with naming recognition has a long and colorful history. Ancient societies built temples to the leaders who provided for them; the names of ancient Egyptian and Sumerian rulers are still with us today because their names were chiseled on the buildings, arches, tablets, and monuments they built. Will the names engraved in stone on our schools, museums, and libraries remain to inform and impress those who come after us? No wonder our donors are motivated to give! We promise them their own personal legacy by agreeing to honor their names *in perpetuity* with future generations.

Planning Donor Benefits

In more recent years, the IRS has weighed in to make sure that charitable gifts are not being traded for items of value. Nonprofits are required to provide a receipt for all gifts above a minimal value, certifying that the donor has received "no goods or services" in exchange for the gift. Anything of value accepted by the donor in return for the contribution—such as attendance at an annual donor dinner—must be subtracted from the value of the gift deduction declared by the donor to the IRS.

Due to these limits on giving donors a quid pro quo, as well as the age-old longing of humans for their names to live beyond their lifetimes, a sophisticated barter system has developed: Public recognition has become the accepted medium offered by nonprofit organizations to their donors in return for making a major gift (see Exhibit 7.1).

How much recognition is enough? The basic advice for recognition is the same that underlies every other activity with major gifts: *Know your donors*. For some donors, you can never do enough. Every organization has donors who require serious handholding. They may be looking for the illumination of their name, at night, with big lights and very large lettering. Some donors have begun to execute contracts with nonprofits that outline, to the nearest decimal point, the size and typeface that will be used to engrave their name on "their" building. In some cases, these donors require firm handling to ensure that the building or the program they fund actually meets the needs of *the nonprofit*, not the donor.

EXHIBIT 7.1

4 Basic Rules of Donor Recognition

1. Don't create recognition benefits that will jeopardize the donor's charitable gift deduction.

2. Develop a standard package of recognition opportunities with prices established prior to starting solicitations.

3. Settle recognition issues during the solicitation call or shortly thereafter.

4. Confirm the way the donor wishes to have her name appear in writing.

At the other end of the spectrum are donors who simply don't need or desire recognition. Some have been honored enough through a lifetime of philanthropic giving, while others may just be modest. There are donors who prefer to operate below the radar and don't want to be known publicly as targets for every organization in their communities. Every nonprofit will encounter a few donors who wish to remain anonymous. (Sometimes, due to list sorting in development information systems that spew out donor names, anonymity requires more staff attention than providing recognition does.)

Family foundation trustees, who may be second- or third-generation family members, or trusted family advisors giving away accumulated wealth often are the donors least attracted to recognition benefits. Their role in selecting appropriate beneficiaries is focused more on the goals and purposes the foundation is committed to meeting. Yet even when giving away someone else's money, it can be fun and rewarding for trustees to participate in the acclaim and honor accorded to major donors. The best way to learn what recognition each donor expects is to ask, preferably during or immediately after the solicitation process.

Rather than making up or negotiating recognition plans on an ad hoc basis, it is better to develop a standard package of benefits and recognition opportunities that can be presented to all major donors. Addressing recognition issues openly during the solicitation meeting can help to determine whether the donor's wishes can be met. In general, if it's legal, not too expensive, and doesn't prove unfair to those who made gifts of equal value, you should try to meet the donor's wishes.

If a donor requests a change or addition to the organization's approved recognition benefits, then that request should go to the group that makes advancement policy: the board or the development committee. Always instruct volunteer solicitors to refer issues back to the group that determines policy; this way, the onus for approval is taken off them, and the nonprofit can deal fairly and equitably with all major donors at the same level.

Donor recognition and benefit programs at nonprofits are multiplying as a way of attracting more and larger gifts. It is preferable to design recognition programs that are made up of benefits that accrue to the donor without any matching devaluation of the charitable gift deduction by the IRS. This means that the benefits offered cannot have any fair market financial value. Attractive benefits such as free cruises, free tickets, and free black-tie donor dinners now have to be accompanied by a declared fair market value, so that donors can subtract this value from their gift when declaring the amount eligible for a charitable deduction. Accountants may love these extras, but donors definitely do not.

Capital Naming Options

In the past decade, the plethora of capital campaigns has pushed naming opportunities to the limit. Named spaces include everything from the cloakroom to bathroom sinks. Any organization new to capital campaigns can visit the local hospital, community center, or private university for a hands-on guide to naming options. Most interior rooms can carry names; common naming options include classrooms, galleries, offices, labs, entryways, lobbies, suites, conference rooms, and public spaces. In naming interior spaces, it has become common to have the name recognized on a plaque or sign near or in the space that the donor "bought" with his gift, as well as engraving the name on a central plaque that holds an overall list of all building donors, located near the building entrance or in a highly visible public space (see Exhibit 7.2).

Exterior building naming opportunities provide more visibility for the donor, cost more, and usually provide the lead gift in a capital campaign. Some campaign consultants recommend that a set percentage of the total cost of the building be used to price the exterior name; this amount can range from 30% to more than 50% of the building's cost, including furnishings and equipment. For instance, for a new museum wing that will cost $10 million, the exterior naming price might be set anywhere from $3 million to $5 million.

 RULES OF THE ROAD

Don't choose your campaign chair just for her money, but don't choose one without it either.

EXHIBIT 7.2

Sample Naming Options for a $3M Capital Campaign

Name of Building (exterior)	$1,500,000
Main Entrance/Atrium Lobby	$ 500,000
Conference Room	$ 350,000
Computer Center	$ 250,000
Administrative Suite	$ 200,000
Laboratory I	$ 150,000
Laboratory II	$ 150,000
Classroom I	$ 50,000
Classroom II	$ 50,000
Classroom III	$ 50,000
Faculty Office I	$ 25,000
Faculty Office II	$ 25,000
Total	**$3,300,000**

Factors to assess when setting the price of exterior naming recognition opportunities include:

- The size of the overall campaign and the total dollars needed

- The cost of the building

- The giving capacity of the prospects available

- The comparative pricing of similar naming options in your region

- The ability to raise the remainder of the money needed

Visibility issues such as exterior signage, lighting, and the size and placement of the name should be cleared with the donor during the planning stages. If these issues could pose a threat to the big gift, it is wise to bring them up during the initial solicitation, to avoid the risk of offending a major donor later.

External naming options also can include portions of a larger complex; hospitals, museums, and schools often name wings, pavilions, quadrangles, outdoor recreation facilities, sculpture gardens, and even the entire campus in return for large gifts.

Landscaped areas, including gardens, courtyards, entryways, paths, benches, and bridges, also can be named. If it is financially feasible to raise money by naming these areas without targeting the funds for capital improvements, consider using these gifts as sources for endowment for upkeep and maintenance of building and grounds.

Setting the price levels for naming options is ultimately a function of the community, its wealth, and the prospect base. If you price a new building name at $2 million, because the total need is $4 million, and your top prospect is capable of giving only $1 million, your project is in trouble. Consider dropping the exterior name back to $1 million and increasing the number of interior naming options to make up the difference. Or design the building with two exterior wings that can be named for $500,000 each, in addition to the main structure that will be named for $1 million.

It is also important to consider the going market price for comparable buildings realized by other nonprofits in the region. This is one area of advancement in which *a rising tide carries all boats*: If the biggest campaign in your region just received a $5 million gift for the exterior naming of a new building, it becomes easier for your organization to price your new building (of comparable size and visibility) at $5 million. In general, capital campaign pricing tends to be higher on the East Coast and the West Coast, because there is a greater concentration of wealth in these regions, more donors capable of making large gifts, and a higher cost for building construction.

The price of a naming option is not necessarily tied directly to the cost of that specific space. The basic rule of thumb for pricing capital naming options is that the most visible, attractive spaces bring the highest price. Thus, the main entryway, which might cost $20,000 to construct, could be priced at $100,000 because everyone entering the building will pass through it. Remember that the donor is not literally buying square footage; you might charge $250,000 for the 200-square-foot main conference room on the first floor and only $50,000 for the 800-square-foot classroom on the third floor.

Most capital campaigns price their naming options so that when the prices for all of the spaces are added up, the total sum is from 5 to 10% more than the dollar total needed to fully fund the facility. This is done because not all of the naming

TIPS & TECHNIQUES

Naming Opportunities and Capital Projects

- Develop a price list in advance.

- You do not need to tie the pricing of a naming option directly to the cost of that specific area in a capital project.

- Have the price list reviewed and approved by your board, executive director, and major gift or campaign volunteer committee.

- Learn what level of pricing is marketable in your community by visiting other nonprofits conducting capital campaigns.

- Use good taste—don't put bathrooms or wiring closets on the list.

- Test your prices and options with prospects before you ask.

- Don't promise to name spaces that aren't in the final plans.

- All the naming options should add up to 5 to 10% more than the goal.

options may be sold. Some areas prove to be more popular than others, and it is difficult to predict ahead of time what gift levels will prove to be most popular with donors.

Furthermore, many capital projects experience cost creep, where due to architectural changes, market increases in the price of materials, or the added expense of interior furnishings, the cost increases from the original projections. Plan to raise a little more money from the beginning as a practical way to cover these cost increases, which often arise months or years into the project.

Endowments: Recognition in Perpetuity

Endowment giving is an altogether different ballgame from capital giving. Endowment donors are making a gift in which the original gift amount is held as the principal and is invested for long-term growth. Only the interest income is spent on the program or area determined by the donor at the time the gift is made. Usually endowment investment and expenditures are handled through board policy, and by policy a certain percentage of income or interest is set for annual expenditures. In recent years, annual endowment expenditures have been set in the range of 4 to 5% of the total invested (see Exhibit 7.3).

Endowments are given, at least theoretically, in perpetuity. Legal action is required to release the principal in order to allow it to be spent or for the use to be changed. Examples of circumstances that require legal action might include: bankruptcy, the pending closure of the organization, or a major change or threat to the institution's continued existence. A change of governance might qualify, for instance; recently, when some hospitals that had nonprofit status were bought by for-profit corporations, their endowments were restructured into foundations and used for purposes other than those that the donors had originally specified.

Endowment donors are interested in recognition, but often that recognition is expressed in a different manner than that for capital donors. Endowment donors tend to be more interested in the long-term health and success of the organization than in having a space with their name on it. Donors of endowed gifts often are offered naming options that reflect the areas where their money will be used. These areas tend to gravitate toward programs, positions, departments, schools, workshops, lectureships, and other elements of the nonprofit's work rather than to physical spaces.

Often the nonprofit will set a floor for endowing an area and receiving naming recognition. The most common levels set for the base endowed gifts are $10,000

EXHIBIT 7.3	
Sample Endowment Payouts Calculated at 5%	
An endowed gift of:	**Produces annual income stream of:**
$10,000	$500
$100,000	$5,000
$250,000	$12,500
$500,000	$25,000
$1,000,000	$50,000

or $25,000; which level you select is most likely a factor of the capacity and willingness of your donor base to make larger gifts. A first-time endowment effort might start at the lower end. The reason for setting a base level for endowed gifts is that, due to the nature of the gift, only the interest is being spent on an annual basis. Thus, a gift of $10,000, invested to produce 5% annually, is going to offer the institution only $500 per year in expendable funds. This doesn't go very far, so it really isn't worth it to the nonprofit to solicit, manage, offer recognition, and prepare stewardship reports for endowed gifts below this level.

An organization can offer large naming options to both endowment and capital donors in support of a similar purpose. Many universities, for instance, offer both the naming of a school or department, as well as the building in which it will be housed, as a major gift opportunity. In such cases, the school's naming gift often is directed toward the endowment, providing long-term support for faculty, programs, and students, while the building naming gift would cover the cost of construction and furnishings (see Exhibit 7.4).

It is also possible to construct a major gift so that part of it is recognized in the naming of an endowment and another portion is recognized in the naming of a physical space. Usually, when such a gift is structured, the donor is brought into the

---

EXHIBIT 7.4

Endowment Recognition Opportunities for a Museum

Named Position for the Executive Director	$2,000,000
Named Position for a Curator	$1,000,000
Named Position for the Education Director	$500,000
Named Endowment for a Program (depending on program size)	$25,000 to $1,000,000
Named Endowment for a Lecture Series	$250,000 to $500,000
Named Endowment for a Gallery or Hall (depending on collection and needs)	$50,000 to $1,000,000
Named Endowment for Resource Center	$50,000 to $250,000

planning, and the money often follows the use. For instance, if a $1 million gift is made in support of a new social services center, you might allocate $500,000 to construction costs and the remaining $500,000 for an endowment to support service providers. The donor receives recognition for both a capital naming gift with a plaque in an appropriate space, and his name is attached to the program that is being endowed.

Some campaigns now structure all their capital gifts so that a portion of every gift is allocated to endowment. Doing this provides ongoing funds for maintenance and upkeep, which greatly relieves the pressure of adding new facilities to an over-strained budget. In such cases, the nonprofit must make its policies very clear to donors and should prepare a written gift agreement that donors sign to make certain that the use of the funds is clearly defined to avoid misunderstandings. Recognition in the capital project should be given for the total amount donated, even if a portion is to be removed for the permanent endowment.

Because endowments make more of an impact on an institution if they are larger, one helpful strategy is to start working with a donor or a donor family on giving a small endowed fund that can be added to over the span of years or even generations.

You might set your floor for endowed gifts at $10,000, for instance, and name and recognize an initial $10,000 gift from a certain donor for an educational program. The donor, his children, his estate, and even friends or colleagues can direct gifts to the endowed program over time, growing it from a small start-up fund into a large, well-established, and well-endowed program over many years. This strategy is particularly effective with planned giving donors, who can use trusts or bequests to grow their endowment funds substantially.

Endowments are not maintenance-free savings accounts. Many organizations provide extensive stewardship to endowment donors, informing them about investment policies and results as well as providing an annual accounting for funds spent. This is one reason why organizations usually set a floor level for named endowment funds. These issues will be discussed further in the stewardship section in this chapter.

LIVE & LEARN

Beware of Land Mines

The kickoff of the Art Center's campaign was to be a very fancy four-course lunch in a private room at the best restaurant in town. The chair wanted to bring in a high-profile speaker to attract all the top prospects. Luckily, someone had an in with a Hollywood celebrity, and she agreed to come for free. The event quickly sold out.

At noon there was no sign of the actress. She was finally located at her hotel, and by the end of the luncheon, her limo rolled up to the door. Out stumbled the star, clearly inebriated, in a shocking state of disarray. She lurched up to the podium and began to deliver a slurred speech on land mines, Hollywood's latest cause célèbre. The crowd murmured in dismay. After five minutes of incoherent rambling, she was hurriedly ushered off stage.

The chair was mortified as word of the disaster raced through the city. Soon, however, everyone could talk of nothing else, and the lucky ones who had been there and seen it all retold the story with relish. Just as the chair had planned, the event was the hit of the fundraising season, and the campaign turned out to be a huge success.

Pricing Naming and Recognition Opportunities

Beware of the attitude of some nonprofits that *if you build it, they will come.* A good feasibility study, research into the gift levels of other campaigns in your region, and an intimate knowledge of your prospect list will save you the pain of pricing beyond the capability of your donor base. Decisions about pricing the most attractive naming areas affect the entire array of recognition pricing offered from the top down and must be made with foresight and knowledge of the donor prospect pool available.

Gift Tables and Recognition Levels

Recognition prices in major gift drives should be tied to the gift levels on the organization's gift table, which in turn have to be adjusted to the number and level of real prospects identified. Gift tables are development financial planning tools used to help determine the number of gifts needed at each giving level, as well as the size of the gifts needed, to reach the goal that has been set for the drive.

Six steps are involved in setting gift recognition levels:

1. Create a gift table for the desired goal.

2. Determine the highest level gifts needed to meet the goal.

3. Develop naming opportunities and prices that match the gift table in terms of both the number of gifts needed and the levels of gifts needed.

4. Identify and research donors to match the gift levels and numbers of gifts needed at each level.

5. Adjust the gift table and the prices to match the prospects identified.

6. Test the gift table structure and the prices with board members, volunteer leaders, and top prospects.

Gift tables are developed through a combination of art and science. They combine information known about the organization's past giving, its future potential giving, and its identified donor base with the needs and goals at hand. Gift tables usually are constructed from the top down, with the key decision points being how many gifts are needed at the top and what dollar level is potentially available for the leadership gifts at the top of the chart.

Campaign A for $5 million that can identify a leadership gift at $2.5 million will look very different from Campaign B for $5 million with a top leadership gift of $1 million (see Exhibit 7.5). Note that Campaign A only needs to find 15 donors to make its goal, but Campaign B requires more than three times as many donors to raise the same amount of money. Campaign A will be easier to run, less expensive to staff, and more efficient in terms of overhead than Campaign B, but the success of Campaign A depends on the big gift of $2.5 million coming in.

These early projections about donors and gift size are directly related to recognition and the pricing of naming opportunities. For example, Campaign A will price its top recognition opportunity (the exterior name of the new building) at $2.5 million. Campaign B may decide to name the building for $1 million; conversely, it may decide to hold that name for a future donor and offer the name of the main interior entry hall for $1 million.

EXHIBIT 7.5

Top Leadership Gifts for Two Campaigns

Campaign A
Goal is $5,000,000, Largest Gift is $2,500,000

Gift Level	# Prospects Needed	# of Donors Needed	Total $	Cumulative $
$2,500,000	3	1	$2,500,000	$2,500,000
$1,000,000	3	1	$1,000,000	$3,500,000
$ 500,000	3	1	$ 500,000	$4,000,000
$ 250,000	6	2	$ 500,000	$4,500,000
$ 100,000	6	2	$ 200,000	$4,700,000
$ 50,000	12	4	$ 200,000	$4,900,000
$ 25,000	12	4	$ 100,000	$5,000,000
Totals	**45**	**15**	**$5,000,000**	

Campaign B
Goal is $5,000,000, Largest Gift is $1,000,000

Gift Level	# Prospects Needed	# of Donors Needed	Total $	Cumulative $
$1,000,000	3	1	$ 1,000,000	$1,000,000
$ 500,000	9	3	$ 1,500,000	$2,500,000
$ 250,000	12	4	$ 1,000,000	$3,500,000
$ 100,000	15	5	$ 500,000	$4,000,000
$ 50,000	30	10	$ 500,000	$4,500,000
$ 25,000	36	12	$ 300,000	$4,800,000
$ 10,000	60	20	$ 200,000	$5,000,000
Totals	**165**	**55**	**$ 5,000,000**	

Campaign A, with its exterior naming option priced at $2.5 million, fills out the gift table admirably, but if no prospects are available at that level, the campaign will fail dramatically. It is better to be conservative and count on a top gift of $1 million and several at $500,000 (Campaign B) and to achieve the goal, than to miss the top gift and have the whole campaign fail.

Recognition for Major Annual Gifts

Myriad programs offer recognition to donors who make gifts to ongoing programs and annual support. These benefits can be considered to be recognition for major gifts if the annual gift level is $10,000 to $25,000 or higher. In other words, annual giving and major gift giving programs overlap at the point where donors make what would be considered a major gift to an annual giving program.

Many nonprofits organize their annual giving benefit programs into giving clubs, so that larger donors of annual gifts, whether they are giving $10,000 or $25,000, all receive a standardized package of attractive items. These giving clubs, or higher-level donor societies, can make use of their benefits packages to solicit new donors or to move past donors at lower levels up to higher giving levels.

A great deal of thought needs to be put into developing the benefit packages for upper-level giving societies (see Exhibit 7.6). The offerings should be appropriate to the institutional style and ethos as well as meet IRS guidelines. Often, volunteer committees or board development committees are good resources for setting and reviewing these benefit programs.

Examples of items that nonprofits might include in their benefits program for $10,000-level donors to annual operations include*:

- Use of the organization's facilities at no charge or a reduced rate

- Background tours or special behind-the-scenes visits

- Exclusive dinners or receptions with donors of a similar level

- Listing at a specific level in the donor honor roll

*Be sure to follow IRS guidelines that require nonprofits to declare the market value of all items and services received by donors, so that they can adjust their charitable deduction accordingly.

EXHIBIT 7.6

Donor Recognition Plan for a Secondary School

Donors of $10,000 to $25,000:

- Name engraved on the permanent Donor Wall (patron level)
- Name on the printed Donor Honor Roll (patron level)
- Name on the donor list on Web site (patron level)
- Autographed book with bookplate
- Invitation to headmaster's reception for major donors

Donors of $25,000 to $100,000:

- Name engraved on the permanent Donor Wall (pillar level)
- Name on the printed Donor Honor Roll (pillar level)
- Name on the donor list on Web site (pillar level)
- Autographed book with bookplate
- Invitation to headmaster's reception for major donors
- Two tickets to the annual black tie fundraising event

Donors of $100,000 to $250,000:

- Name engraved on the permanent Donor Wall (headmaster's level)
- Name on the printed Donor Honor Roll (headmaster's level)
- Name on the donor list on Web site (headmaster's level)
- Autographed book with bookplate
- Invitation to reception for major donors
- Four tickets to the annual black tie fundraising event

continued on next page

EXHIBIT 7.6 CONTINUED

Donors of $250,000 to $1,000,000:

- Name engraved on the permanent Donor Wall (chairman's level)

- Name on the printed Donor Honor Roll (chairman's level)

- Name on the Donor list on Web site (chairman's level)

- Autographed book with bookplate

- Invitation to reception for major donors

- Exclusive dinner with chairman of board and donors of $250,000+

- Free table at the annual black tie fundraising event

Donors of $1,000,000 and more:

- Name engraved on the permanent Donor Wall (founder's level)

- Name on the printed Donor Honor Roll (founder's level)

- Name on the donor list on the Web site (founder's level)

- Autographed book with bookplate

- Invitation to reception for major donors

- Exclusive dinner with chairman of board and donors of $250,000+

- Free table at the annual black tie fundraising event

- Donor profile in the organization's newsletter, community-wide PR, and Web site headline announcing gift (if desired)

- Name placed on a donor wall

- Invitations to special openings, receptions, events, or tours

- Access to experts: artists, teachers, program directors, as appropriate

- Gift items of low value associated with the nonprofit: plaques, pins, framed posters, books, CDs, mugs, T-shirts, ties, scarves, and so on

- Access to special trips, travel, or learning opportunities

Nonprofits also can recognize the names of program sponsors, underwriters, or other donors of one-time gifts for ongoing program support. For instance, if a foundation gives $10,000 for annual support, the nonprofit can find an ongoing program—say, educational outreach to schoolchildren—and provide recognition linking the foundation, the gift, and the program together for one year. This type of recognition allows organizations to solicit, receive, and recognize gifts that ultimately support budget relief, rather than budget enhancement, through large gifts devoted to annual support.

Higher-end annual gift programs often begin to resemble major gift programs in their style of personal solicitation and recognition. Often annual gifts of $5,000, $10,000 and more are personally solicited through a face-to-face meeting, using volunteers and staff, much like a major gifts program. Gifts for events, programs, outreach newsletters, lectures, visiting experts, ongoing conservation, and maintenance can all be "recognized" and carry the name of donors for a year or less. As many organizations find it harder and harder to raise unrestricted dollars that go to support ongoing operations, the strategy of asking for larger annual gifts to be directed to the support of ongoing activities, with appropriate recognition, may be a powerful way to fill budget needs.

Corporate Philanthropic Recognition

Corporate charitable giving has changed dramatically over the past few decades. At one time, corporate leaders made personal choices about charitable support, with much of the money available going to the chief executive's personal interest areas, such as her alma mater or a nonprofit where she served on the board. Giving was often ad hoc, local, and mostly dissociated from the company's business and marketing needs. That model is becoming less common as accountability and fiscal responsibility become the watchwords of corporate philanthropy.

Today, corporate giving often is managed by a committee or made through a separate foundation with its own board. Many public companies now have to answer to their shareholders for the distribution of philanthropic dollars. This doesn't mean that corporate philanthropy is dead; far from it. But company leaders now

Trends in Corporate Giving

A development officer worked hard to strategize how to get a gift from each of the two large, global banks that led the banking industry in her region. With the help of her board members, she secured an appointment with each of the bank's chairmen.

At Bank I, she was told that her nonprofit's 25-year history of banking with them would be the key factor in their decision to support a gift for her program. The bank also was very interested in recognition; it wanted to make gifts that would bring it PR coverage across the community. It pledged $100,000 as major sponsors for the nonprofit's big annual fundraising event.

The chairman of Bank II explained that its giving was now going to programs that would help prepare the diverse urban workforce in the region for professional jobs in finance and industry. He pledged $100,000 toward a program the organization had developed for underperforming high school students. Bank II never even asked if her organization was a customer. (The organization was not; it did all its banking with Bank I.)

Two gifts, two completely different approaches to giving. The key to getting each gift was for the fundraiser to learn what motivated each bank and to find a gift that met each chairman's needs.

target their gifts to communities where their presence will make an impact on workers, their communities, and the organizations that serve them.

Some companies have chosen to target their giving in sectors that match their business interests, such as housing, disaster relief, or health. Others simply make sure that they get as much "bang for their buck" as possible, making demands on nonprofits for enhanced visibility and benefits in return for financial support. Contracts between nonprofits and corporate donors are now more common, spelling out exactly what advertising, public relations (PR), naming rights, and donor benefits are expected. An increased emphasis on marketing and cobranding has stepped up the number of tie-ins between nonprofits and their business partners. In short, corporate giving has become more corporate—more like a business decision than like a philanthropic decision.

Corporate philanthropy also has become more global as the American economy has expanded globally. The non-American boards of huge international companies, such as Shell Oil, are beginning to become more involved in setting giving policy. Much more corporate and foundation money is being directed to global needs, such as health and education in the underdeveloped countries where international companies work, hire, develop natural resources, and sell their products. Those nonprofits that work and deliver services in a global environment may find their potential for corporate support expanding and their recognition needs becoming tied to the international marketplace.

Donor Walls and Honor Rolls

One of the most traditional methods to honor donors is to put their name on a donor plaque or donor wall, or to distribute a printed list with donor names. Firms that produce creative displays for donor walls and plaques are a mainstay of fundraising convention exhibition halls, with a number of attractive products on the market. Some nonprofits opt to list donors by levels, with larger donor names in larger type; others, sensitive to the need to be tactful in small communities, feel that all donors should be listed in the same size type without discrimination. Each institution should consider the manners, style, and precedents of its own community when planning donor recognition.

Honor rolls were once a mainstay of donor recognition programs. Now many nonprofits produce lists on their Web site to save on paper and printing costs. Electronic banners, donor lists, and virtual annual reports are all ways to offer donor recognition without the additional costs of print communication. Assess your donor base before dropping all print communication; older, more traditional, and less affluent donor groups might still prefer to see their name in print as opposed to online recognition.

If you do decide to print, consider printing your donor honor roll as an insert or section of a printed piece that you already produce to save time and money. Honor rolls can be inserted into newsletters, annual reports, printed programs (for events), magazines, or mailed separately bound. Some organizations use a draft of the honor roll as a last-chance solicitation piece, but this is probably more appropriate for annual fund gifts than for major gift fundraising. *Make sure that your donors have given you permission to print their names*—printing the names of donors who asked to remain anonymous is a sure way to lose friends.

Stewardship for the Next Gift

Many major donors keep giving gifts throughout their lifetime to the same organization. If making their gifts is personally satisfying and if the organization continues to meet needs that they, as donors, find compelling and meaningful, then the giving relationship is one that benefits both sides. Creating a lifetime giving relationship can be very rewarding to both donors and the institution. It saves time and money for the charitable organization, which doesn't have to spend money and staff time to find new donors, and it provides a way for the donor to see progress and development in furthering his causes. The key to making such long-term relationships work is to provide good stewardship.

Creating a Stewardship Plan

Good stewardship is more than just thanking a donor appropriately, although that is where stewardship begins. It usually encompasses the effort of building and maintaining a strong relationship with the donor after the gift has been received. Good stewardship starts with a plan; in the case of donors at a higher level, making a written plan is the best way to track and keep contact with donors in the face of changing institutional priorities and staffing.

The written stewardship plan should cover activities with the top 10% of your current donor base, whether these donors give at the $1,000 or the $1 million level.

A stewardship program has three goals:

1. *To provide appropriate recognition and thanks for the gift.* All donors need to be thanked promptly and appropriately. For most major gift donors, this means a letter or call from the executive director of the nonprofit. Additional thank-you contacts from leaders on the board, staff members involved in the gift, and volunteer leaders are also welcome.

RULES OF THE ROAD

Few donors are insulted by being asked for more than they can give.

Make sure that the information in such letters is accurate but not too personal. Volunteers, for instance, can know the level of the gift but should not be given confidential information about trusts, payment plans, and pledge details. Many universities now ask students participating in their annual giving call programs to make thank-you calls to annual fund donors; consider having those who make such calls take a night to thank major gift donors also.

With larger donors, especially in capital or endowment campaigns where naming opportunities have been offered, plan to have an advancement professional make a stewardship call on the donor to review recognition plans. The caller can review signage, the wording on plaques and donors walls, and double check spelling and amounts. It is possible to use such a stewardship call to increase the size of the gift, by talking to the donor about remaining naming options that are still open that might be more attractive than the one the donor originally selected. Like most contacts with major donors, it is preferable to make such a visit in person, if at all possible.

2. *To keep the donor informed about the use of her money.* The donor made the gift expecting the money to be used wisely and efficiently to produce results. Nothing makes a major donor more pleased with her gift than timely and appropriate reporting on the results of putting that gift to use. In some nonprofits, this kind of stewardship might mean putting a face to the services rendered; identifying the number of meals served, students educated, or homes provided for the needy can help to build ties to the donor. This type of information can be delivered in a letter, newsletter, or a personal visit to follow up with the donor.

Consider ways to bring the donor closer to the organization and to the actual work going on. Offer the donor a chance to make personal contact with those who are served by the organization. Scholarship donors, for instance, often are invited to events where they can meet and mingle with students attending the institution on scholarships.

If the donor gave to a capital project, make sure that she is invited to any dedication or event provided to open the building. Events that provide recognition for specific programs or buildings should include all donors to those areas. Consider offering personal, smaller recognition ceremonies, held before or after the main dedication ceremony, to thank donors whose gifts reach a certain level. Make sure to include major sponsors and donors when producing honor rolls, plaques, programs, and dedication speeches at such events.

3. *To apprise the donor of organizational needs and new priorities—that is, to cultivate her for the next gift.* It is a truism in development that the best donors are those who are already giving to your organization. The effort to keep their loyalty is the real goal of stewardship. Remember that stewardship is the act of reporting on the last gift, but it often lays the groundwork for the next gift. Donors can be kept up to date with a nonprofit where they have made a major investment in a wide variety of ways.

Newsletters, annual reports, honor rolls, magazines, and Web sites are all appropriate spaces to provide updates for donors. Some larger organizations produce a development newsletter, semiannually or quarterly, that focuses on stewardship and donor recognition. Others devote pages in their alumni or membership journals to development and financial reports to keep readers up to date.

Once again, the personal approach works best with larger donors. Face-to-face stewardship visits can allow for continuous donor cultivation and education. Some donors will indicate that they are ready to commit to another gift, or add to the one they have recently made, if they are visited with regularly. Others will be more willing to make a new gift at the end of their pledge period, when their gift is paid off, if they understand the needs of the organization more fully. Time spent with current donors is time well spent.

Keeping Records and Financial Reporting

Good stewardship involves careful record keeping. Meet regularly with your financial staff to understand and coordinate what records they keep on donors, pledge payments, trusts, endowments, and investment returns. These responsibilities should be discussed and assigned so that follow-up and recording issues are settled before problems arise:

- Who will produce, check, and mail pledge reminders?

- Who will credit pledge payments to the correct account?

- Who will track and follow up with delinquent donors?

- Who will keep original gift agreements, contracts, signed pledge documents, and other documentation that is necessary for tracking gift issues years down the line?

- Who will track endowment donations, set up endowed accounts, credit gifts to these accounts, and determine the payout and expenditures from endowed accounts?

- Who will handle stewardship with endowment donors, updating them on the status of their accounts and the expenditures made from each account?

Endowment donors are entitled to a different type of stewardship from major gift donors who give through cash or pledges. Most organizations track endowment investment and earnings through their financial offices, and each endowment donor should be apprised on an annual basis of the status of the endowment account. This should include the amount of the original principal given and invested; the growth of the account from reinvested interest, earnings, and accrued value; and the annual expenditure amount with an indication of how the money expended was used.

To be completely transparent, many nonprofits distribute detailed reports on investment practices, short- and long-term growth rates, and the names of firms used to invest the endowment portfolio. These decisions are policy matters that should be considered by both the finance and the development committees of the board.

Planned gift arrangements also require regular communication and interaction between development and finance staff members. Adhering to bequest restrictions, managing trusts and their investment, and deciding how and when to sell donated stocks and bonds are all part of the chief financial officer's portfolio. However, many times the development staff members hold the key to the relationship with the donor, besides having physical ownership of most of the relevant documentation. Both sides must keep the door open to good communication and trust to serve the donor well.

Because of the need to keep important donors happy, a strong working relationship between development and finance staff members is necessary when dealing with complex gifts and reporting policies. The major donor who is satisfied that her money is being invested properly, used according to her wishes, and efficiently administered will be more likely to make the next big gift down the road.

When to Ask Again

Some donors are ready to give more as soon as the initial amount of their gift is negotiated. It may seem unlikely, or even unwise, to ask a recent major gift donor to think about giving again, but there are certain cases where a second ask can be very successful. Circumstances such as the ones highlighted in "Tips & Techniques" could hint that a major donor might be willing to make a new gift, or add to her prior gift, within one year of making her first gift.

The most common time to approach a past major gift donor for a new gift is just before the pledge period has ended for her most recent gift. Many major gift offices track pledge timetables for this reason, so that they can systematically plan to revisit former donors and begin the discussion of a new gift. This may also be a time when planned giving, which usually involves the development of a longer, lifetime relationship with the donor, is most appropriate to bring into the discussion.

When Can a Donor Be Asked for a Second Gift?

1. When the first large gift is paid off all at once or when a pledge made over several years is paid off.

2. When the first gift comes nowhere near the capacity of the donor, and the donor continues to be engaged in the work of the nonprofit.

3. When the first gift was made for a naming opportunity in a capital campaign and, near the end of the campaign, there are other more attractive (and more expensive) naming options remaining.

4. When a challenge or matching gift program is put in place that the donor might be able to respond to.

5. When a project close to the donor's heart is nearing completion, the donor can be asked to close the gap between what is needed and the goal.

Summary

Building a relationship with major gift donors goes well beyond the standard cultivation and solicitation activities. What the nonprofit provides in donor service through recognition programs, donor clubs, naming opportunities, benefits, and honor rolls can impact both the size of the gift and whether it will be repeated. Donors who enjoy a long-term relationship with the organization, are kept updated on the use of their funds, and are visited now and then by staff to keep them current with the nonprofit's needs, are much more likely to give again.

Transparent financial reporting, which depends on keeping a good relationship with the finance office staff, is also a basic building block of good stewardship. Deciding how and what to report to donors should be a board policy matter, but keeping major donors involved and happy with their investment in the nonprofit enterprise falls squarely on the advancement staff. Making a second ask, or asking a donor to increase a first gift, is also an advancement office decision.

The willingness of the donor to contribute another gift to the organization has to be reviewed on an individual basis and depends on a variety of factors, such as financial wherewithal, pledge timetables, recognition opportunities, and the donor's own commitment to the organization and its needs. Like so much in major gift work, each donor must be dealt with as an individual, with her own unique interests, needs, and capabilities considered and acted on.

CHAPTER 8

Special Opportunities in Major Gifts

After reading this chapter you will be able to:

- Integrate planned giving into your major gift program
- Raise major gifts in a capital campaign
- Prepare for mega gifts

Planned Giving in a Major Gift Program

Many of the largest major gifts actually arrive as planned gifts. All major gift officers should be trained and updated on planned giving tools in order to make the best of opportunities that may arise unexpectedly with donors. Major gift donors often make more than one gift during their lifetime of involvement with an organization, and in some cases the "ultimate" gift will be a planned gift. It should be a long-term goal of major gift work to bring donors to the point where the feasibility of a planned gift can be discussed. Planned gifts also can be a method of increasing the size of a major gift, especially in cases where a gift made from income, or a gift that requires a cash outlay, might result in a more limited dollar amount.

Fundraising through planned giving does not have to be conducted solely by a professional who specializes in trusts and estate planning. Major gift officers who are properly trained and who keep up to date on the various elements of planned giving can begin the process by introducing the topic to potential donors. The nonprofit staffer does have to be careful not to offer specific legal or financial advice to donors; however, it is appropriate for development staff members to familiarize donors with various types of planned giving tools and thus to help donors learn the benefits and limits of each different type of giving arrangement (see Exhibit 8.1). In some cases, learning about new giving tools might help donors to support the nonprofit in a different manner from what they are contemplating, and could actually bring benefits to donors.

In most cases, sophisticated donors will have their own legal, financial, and estate planning experts to attend to their needs. The role of the major gift officer is to encourage, educate, supply information, and support the intent of donors, not to write trusts, wills, or work on tax returns.

Do not act as the donor's legal or financial advisor. Doing so can become the basis for a conflict-of-interest lawsuit if relatives feel that the nonprofit has taken advantage of a too-willing donor. The IRS and the Securities and Exchange Commission also take a dim view of charitable organizations acting as investment and tax advisors.

EXHIBIT 8.1

Planned Gifts Offer Many Advantages

- Planned gifts allow donors to make larger gifts than might be possible during their lifetime.

- Planned gifts allow donors the use of their funds during their lifetime for unforeseeable needs.

- Planned gifts often allow donors to realize tax advantages.

- Planned gifts can increase retirement income, depending on the vehicle selected.

- Planned gifts can be used to establish an endowed fund to honor a loved one in perpetuity.

- Planned gifts can allow donors to pass assets to heirs at a lower transfer tax cost.

What counts most is the donor's intent to give. This is, in turn, propelled by the quality of the relationship between the donor, the major gift staff member, and the nonprofit. If the intent to give is there, the use of planned giving is just one tool that the major gift staff member has available to make the gift work for the donor and for the organization.

How to Recognize a Planned Giving Prospect

Planned giving prospects are surprisingly easy to find—they exist all over, even among potential donors who might not consider themselves wealthy. This is because planned gifts are usually gifts made from assets, not gifts from income or cash reserves. It is superficial, and ultimately foolhardy, to assume that people who don't look wealthy can't make planned gifts. Often those who spend the least have money saved up somewhere.

IN THE REAL WORLD

Where There Is a Will (or an Insurance Policy), There Is a Way

Two professors, married to each other for 40 years, worked at the same institution. After the husband passed away, the wife wanted to create an endowed chair, both to memorialize her husband and to assure that work would go on in his field of research.

Neither had any wealth beyond the usual faculty retirement funds, but both were passionately committed to furthering research in their chosen field of study. Madame Professor knew that she could never save enough to make a gift or a bequest to fund a chair, which required an endowment of $1 million.

She refused to give up. Although she was approaching late middle age, she was in good health, so she shopped around and bought two life insurance policies to underwrite the chair.

Within two years Madame suffered a massive heart attack and passed away, with the insurance policies paying to fund the chair almost immediately. Her husband's name lives on to support his area of research, just as she desired.

Astonishing stories have emerged as part of development lore of people who had no apparent means who left huge bequests to charity. A few years ago, there was the famous example of the Mississippi laundress who had saved hundreds of thousands of dollars over a lifetime of manual labor. It all went to charity. Recently in New Orleans an older Jewish man left over $1 million when he died to restore his synagogue. His fellow congregants thought he was indigent.

Due to the wide array of vehicles and options in the planned gift arena, planned giving donors come in all shapes and sizes. Little old ladies with large investment portfolios make wonderful planned giving donors. Entrepreneurs who have taken their company public make wonderful planned giving donors. Couples who have

TIPS & TECHNIQUES

Helpful Hints to Find Planned Giving Donors

If you hear a donor say:

- I am planning to retire in the next year

- I am working on my estate plans

- I need my money to support my child, who is handicapped

- I want to make sure my wife is taken care of after I'm gone

he is a potential planned giving donor.

If you know that he has:

- A second home he no longer uses regularly

- A company he started about to go public

- An income stream from rental property

- A 401(k) or other tax-deferred retirement account

- A primary residence that will not be needed by his heirs

he is a potential planned giving donor.

tired of their second home and want to get tax advantages for giving away property make wonderful planned giving donors. And anyone who has made—or plans to make—a will is a wonderful planned giving donor.

Types of Planned Gifts

Sometimes nonprofits, as well as donors, think of planned giving as providing a long-term benefit to the organization only through bequests and charitable trusts. Although such gifts can be very valuable to the organization, they are often underrated because organizations have pressing needs now and want gifts that can be used now.

It is important to remember that many planned gifts can be structured for use immediately, to provide current cash for projects under way (see Exhibit 8.2). These gifts include real estate, stocks, and bonds; assigning a stream of royalties to the nonprofit; and donating works of art or other real property (if the nonprofit is able to sell them).

Some charitable trusts, such as lead trusts, can provide income right away. The charitable lead trust is the mirror image of the more common charitable remainder trust. In the lead trust, the donor transfers assets to a trust that pays income to the nonprofit for a set number of years, then at the end of the trust period, the assets go to the donor's heirs.

The charitable lead trust is even more bankable than a pledge, because it is a legally binding document that assures an income stream to the nonprofit over the life of the trust. For this reason, charitable lead trusts are especially valuable in capital campaigns, where cash flow needs to be assured. (This vehicle is complex to create and administer and requires outside legal advice; it is most useful for donors of six- or seven-figure gifts.)

Other planned gifts are focused on the long term. Working with these gifts can bring powerful resources down the road to the nonprofit, because often the largest philanthropic gifts are made through bequests and trusts. Bequests are probably the easiest planned giving vehicle to understand (see Exhibit 8.3). The donor, if she has a will, can add a codicil making a gift to the nonprofit. If she doesn't have a will, encouraging her to create one is of lasting benefit to her entire family.

EXHIBIT 8.2

Types of Planned Gifts

I. Provide Funds to the Nonprofit for Current Use

- *Charitable Lead Trust*—provides a stream of income over a period of years to the nonprofit; the assets revert to the beneficiaries at the end of the trust period.

- *Real Estate* (gifted, then sold by the nonprofit)

- *Gifts of Marketable Securities* (stocks or bonds)

- *Dedicated Income Stream from Royalties or Rental Income*

- *Donated Art or Other Real Property* (gifted, then sold by the nonprofit)

II. Provide Funds to the Nonprofit on a Deferred Basis

- *Charitable Remainder Trust*—provides a stream of income over a period of years to the income beneficiary; the assets go to the nonprofit at the end of the trust period.

- *Charitable Gift Annuity*—donor makes a gift; nonprofit agrees to pay an income stream to the donor for life; nonprofit invests the gift.

- *Bequest or Other Estate Gifts*

- *Most Gifts of Life Insurance*

- *Gifts of Tax Deferred Retirement Plans*

The main advantage of a bequest is that the donor has the full use of her assets during her lifetime. Many older women, who often outlive their husbands, are most comfortable with bequest giving, because it is a vehicle that allows them to be certain that their money will take care of them throughout their life and, if necessary, provide for their final care and medical costs.

Because bequests and wills are subject to change by the donor at any time, most organizations do not announce or grant recognition to this type of gift until it is actually received, meaning that the donor has passed away. See "Tips & Techniques" for some ways to encourage bequest donors to make a major gift during their

EXHIBIT 8.3

All About Bequests

Advantages of Giving Through a Bequest

- A gift through a bequest can be made in any amount.
- Bequests can be added by codicil to a will already drawn up.
- Bequests allow donors the use of the funds during their lifetime.
- Bequests are gifts that are relatively easy to make and to honor.
- Bequests can make a very large impact on an institution.

Types of Bequests

- A specific dollar amount can be identified.
- A percentage of the estate can be named.
- The gift can be a residual interest in the estate.
- The gift can be real property or real estate named in the will.

Uses of Bequests

- Unrestricted (for general use)
- Restricted, for uses such as program support, equipment, facility maintenance, or capital projects
- Establish a named endowed fund in perpetuity
- Add to an existing endowed fund

lifetime and ways to keep them in the fold through active stewardship. As bequests can be changed at any time during the donor's lifetime, it is important for the nonprofit to keep these donors in the fold through ongoing attention and active involvement in the work of the organization.

Charitable gift annuities and charitable remainder trusts are also popular vehicles for donors, because they provide income over the donor's lifetime to him or his beneficiaries. Remainder trusts are useful for providing for a spouse or child who

Recognition for Donors of Planned Gifts

- Most gifts made through bequests are not recognized during the donor's lifetime; that is, until the donor has passed away and the gift is received.

- Talk to donors directly about making a major gift while they are still alive, when they can see the impact that their gift makes on the organization.

- Ask donors if they are willing to enter into an irrevocable giving arrangement, such as a charitable trust.

- Work with endowment donors to set up the endowed account with a smaller gift while the donor is alive, then ask the donor to fully endow the project through a gift in his will.

- Identify future donors of bequests and other planned gifts and recognize them through the establishment of a planned giving society.

- Offer annual recognition to the members of the planned giving society in the annual report, list them on a special donor wall, and invite them to annual events to keep them abreast of the organization's activities.

needs ongoing support. These vehicles, which are commonly known as life income plans, do have some cost for the nonprofit, which must pay the annuity or, in the case of the trust, won't receive the money until after the beneficiaries have passed away. If well invested, however, these instruments can earn money in the long term for the nonprofit.

Gifts of insurance and tax-deferred retirement plans are also popular forms of delayed, or deferred, giving. Insurance and retirement plan gifts have the advantage of requiring less legal advice; the donor can just sign over a policy or make the nonprofit the beneficiary of his retirement plan. Although the tools of the planned giving trade—trusts, bequests, insurance, real estate, annuities—are often complex, the actual concept of giving away something that the donor owns other than cash or pledges is not difficult to grasp and can be explained easily to even financially unsophisticated donors.

How to Talk About Planned Giving

Often the most difficult issue for the major gift officer or volunteer is how to bring up the concept of planned giving in a conversation with a donor. Certainly one would not wish to be crude or to pry too much into a donor's personal estate plans; in our society, many people find talk about or inference of death to be inappropriate. There are some key indications, however, that a donor might find it helpful to consider a planned gift. Some of these indications are covered in "Tips & Techniques."

A good way to introduce the topic of planned giving is to bring up examples of gifts other donors have made. This can be done without naming donors if they have not specifically granted permission to use their names. The nonprofit staff member or volunteer can offer information on planned giving options.

For instance, if the donor is concerned about providing for his wife or child after he is deceased, bring up the charitable remainder trust in this manner:

> *Many of our donors have found that planned gift options have helped them to resolve the same kind of issue you are facing. Can I tell you a little about how the charitable remainder trust works?*

Follow up by talking about the advantages and disadvantages of the type of planned giving arrangement that might work for this donor. Knowing the benefits and advantages of each type of planned gift arrangement, and the appropriate fit for each kind of gift, is an essential skill of the major gift officer.

Another way to bring planned giving to the attention of a donor is to offer to forward information as a follow-up to a visit:

> *I would like to send you something on charitable remainder trusts that might help you to think about how to provide for your wife.*

Tact, the staff member's familiarity with the tools, and knowledge of the donor all enter into the decision about how and when to bring up planned giving in the conversation. The important point is to make sure that major gift officers are trained and prepared to step in when the facts of the situation make one of these tools an appropriate option for donors to consider.

Marketing of Planned Gifts

Planned gifts also are triggered by marketing materials produced by the nonprofit. Several high-quality for-profit companies now offer an extensive array of brochures, pamphlets, Web sites, and newsletters that cover planned gifts. Stories, examples, and information are all offered in layman's language.

Your organization can personalize these materials so that they look like they were created in-house. With the help of these sophisticated marketing materials, you can produce a planned giving program without actually having the technical support of a lawyer or planned giving specialist on your staff.

Interactive planned giving Web sites, like those offered by Stelter and Company (see www.stelter.com), can show donors what tax advantages and benefits might accrue to them, given certain financial parameters that they enter themselves. These Web sites can be linked to an institutional Web site in a seamless manner. Web sites can be coordinated with newsletters to create a continuous array of planned giving information.

The most effective combination of marketing efforts in planned giving is to combine direct mail, Web site support, and response cards or responsive e-mails from the prospects. Focus in your materials on presenting one or two giving vehicles at a time; don't try to cover the whole array of planned gift options in one mailing or article. Bequests, insurance gifts, and gifts from retirement plan assets are all relatively easy to present and explain, for instance, and might be presented in sequential pieces.

 RULES OF THE ROAD

To find out how much a man is worth, ask his ex-wife.

TIPS & TECHNIQUES

Gifts of Retirement Plan Assets*

A nonprofit can be named as a beneficiary of a donor's IRA, tax-sheltered annuity, Keogh plan, 401(k), or other qualified pension and profit-sharing plans.

Advantages of Giving Through Retirement Plan Assets

- This type of gift is easy to execute: Simply name the nonprofit as a beneficiary of the plan.

- The funds pass to the nonprofit outside of probate and free of all taxes.

- Retirement plan giving provides both estate and income tax savings.

- This form of giving may be better for heirs than giving through a bequest because of the tax advantages.

Note: This area of estate planning may be subject to change through several pieces of legislation pending in Congress. Check with an attorney or tax expert before giving advice to donors.

Another effective marketing tool is to find real-life examples of planned gifts that have been made to your institution and profile those donors in newsletters, mailings, and on Web sites. Use donors who have made planned gifts to help explain the advantages that accrued to them in their own words. Create a planned giving donor society to recognize those who have made gifts to your organization through their estate plans. Finally, make sure that all inquiries are followed up on personally by a staff member. Built correctly, a planned giving program integrated with a major gift program can provide ongoing assets for years to come for your organization.

Major Gifts and Capital Campaigns

Raising major gifts through a capital or endowment campaign can be an effective way to build in the sense of urgency and focus required to help supporters think about and commit to larger gifts. Campaigns can galvanize boards, volunteers, staff, and donors alike. Campaigns also develop a momentum that creates excitement for potential supporters, encourages them to participate at the highest level, and brings satisfaction as the goals are reached.

Campaign Structure and Tools

Campaigns often follow a common structure that makes it easier for the nonprofit to promote major gift giving. Most nonprofits prepare campaign fundraising tools and materials that major gift staff and volunteers can use to raise funds during a campaign. Campaigns usually are organized around a specific project or a set of needs, providing a common focus point for funders and volunteers alike.

Many campaigns start with a feasibility or assessment study, often defined as a set of interviews with potential donors conducted by an outside consultant. These studies can be useful when preparing a campaign plan. Many organizations use these studies to interview or assess the interest and capability of their major gift prospects before entering into a campaign. Prospects who are likely to give large gifts usually respond well to being asked for their advice, and the campaign feasibility study is an appropriate vehicle to use to ask for their input.

Conduct a campaign feasibility study to:

- Determine if the campaign goal is feasible

- Educate the board and volunteers about campaign issues

- Cultivate potential campaign donors by asking for their advice

- Get a feeling for the giving level of potential donors

- Test the case with donors for why the campaign is necessary

- Identify new donors or new groups of donors

- Uncover potential problems or challenges

- Identify potential campaign leaders and volunteers

There are many components to capital campaign planning, and most organizations new to the process will want to seek professional help, either from a consultant or by hiring staff members with campaign experience. A good campaign plan (see Exhibit 8.4) will help the organization bring together all of its stakeholders: board members, volunteer leaders, current donors, and potential prospects. Staff and executive leaders work in better coordination during the campaign if roles are spelled out, timetables are followed, and key components of the campaign strategy are agreed on ahead of time.

Gift tables often are developed as a tool to use during capital campaign planning. These tables are pyramid-style charts that show the number and level of gifts needed to make the campaign goal. Although gift tables sometimes are criticized as pie-in-the-sky efforts at wishful thinking, they do serve several useful purposes.

EXHIBIT 8.4

Components of a Capital Campaign Plan

- Analysis of the strengths and weaknesses of the proposed campaign
- Results of the feasibility study, if one was conducted
- A list of campaign prospects of $10,000+ with suggested ask amounts
- Recommendation on structure of the campaign committee, cochairs, and names of potential volunteers
- Assessment of campaign case, themes, and recommendations on campaign materials that are needed
- Gift table showing the projected size and number of gifts needed
- List of naming opportunities with suggested prices
- Campaign timetable with suggested phases, interim goals, and key events, such as when to go public
- Internal goals for accountability and measurement purposes
- Staffing and budget plan for campaign activity

Uses for Campaign Gift Tables

1. *Use gift tables to sight-raise with board and volunteer leaders.* Learning that a campaign requires a top-level gift of $1 million to succeed can have a galvanizing effect on board members. It may lead them to think of new prospects, to raise the level of their own gifts, or to think about ways to restructure the organization's needs.

2. *Use gift tables to set recognition levels and price naming opportunities.* Campaigns should match the levels and number of gifts needed on the gift table to the prices and number of naming options available for recognition. If the campaign calls for a lead gift of $1 million, there should be a very attractive, appropriate naming opportunity at that level.

3. *Use gift tables to determine if the organization has enough prospects to make the campaign goal.* Use a three-to-one or four-to-one ratio of prospects to gifts needed. Plug in the names of prospects who have the capacity to give at each level on the gift table. This is a good tool to help a nonprofit know if it has the prospects and giving capacity available to reach the goal. If not, either do additional work on identifying new prospects or cut back the size of the campaign.

4. *Use gift tables on calls with major prospects to help "frame" the ask.* Experienced solicitors like to use gift tables to show donors where the gift that they are being asked for sits. This provides a context for the donor, illustrates leadership giving in a concrete way, and allows solicitors to talk about other donors who have given gifts at the same or similar levels.

In the gift table in Exhibit 8.5 for a $2 million capital campaign, the largest gift is set at $500,000. One gift is required at that level. The organization is looking for at least three prospects who are capable of making a gift of that level in order to make a leadership gift. Even if the interest level of the top prospect identified isn't yet confirmed, it is important to begin thinking about who that donor might be, because cultivation for the leadership gift has to start immediately, even before the campaign is begun. If a donor of $500,000 is not found, the campaign will have two choices: either find more donors at the $250,000 and $100,000 levels or cut back the overall size of the campaign.

EXHIBIT 8.5

Campaign Gift Table: Goal of $2 Million, Largest Gift at $500,000

Gift Level	# Prospects Needed	# of Donors Needed	Total $	Cumulative $
$500,000	3	1	$ 500,000	$ 500,000
$250,000	6	2	$ 500,000	$1,000,000
$150,000	3	1	$ 150,000	$1,150,000
$100,000	12	4	$ 400,000	$1,550,000
$ 50,000	15	5	$ 250,000	$1,800,000
$ 25,000	18	6	$ 150,000	$1,950,000
$ 10,000	15	5	$ 50,000	$2,000,000
Totals	**72**	**24**	**$2,000,000**	

One of the advantages of raising major gifts in a capital campaign is that the nonprofit's needs are already identified and very focused. They may include a new building, a renovation of current facilities, or building the endowment. Whatever they encompass, the needs should be laid out clearly and marketed as part of a larger vision of the organization's future. This list of needs, sometimes called the table of needs, becomes the blueprint for campaign volunteers and donors.

Financial planning, including all costs for construction, staffing, added programs, maintenance, and campaign staff, must be completed ahead of time so that volunteers are not surprised with additional funds that have to be raised after the goal is reached. Nothing makes boards and campaign chairs more uneasy—and less attractive to savvy donors—than the appearance of poor financial planning in a capital campaign.

Groundwork for the successful campaign requires the integration of several planning elements: the number and dollar level of gifts available from donors, the cost of the needs of the organization, and the pricing and availability of recognition at the levels that donors are going to give. This means that the gift table, the potential prospect list, and the table of needs with prices all have to be coordinated to make the campaign work. Adding timetables, phases, events, action steps, and marketing plans to this base structure provides the organization the opportunity to flesh out the campaign and to make it more accessible and interesting to donors and volunteers alike.

Once the structure of the campaign is in place, a plan for cultivating the prospects identified can be developed. Doing this will involve a variety of the same techniques used in major gift cultivation.

Common cultivation steps to take with top prospects in a capital campaign include:

- Interviewing top prospects as part of the feasibility study

- Augmenting the board with top prospects (best done before the campaign begins)

- Conducting small-group sessions to explain the needs of the organization

- Holding small-group dinners or other events with top prospects

- Creating a prospect mailing list and developing a communication plan

- Meeting one-on-one in cultivation visits with prospects to assess interest, capability, and opportunities for involvement

- Inviting prospects to kick-off, groundbreaking, dedication, and other campaign-related events

Most organizations find that the hoopla, the external elements of a capital campaign, help to increase interest, engage donors, and bring in new gifts of a size and frequency that would not be possible outside of the framework of the campaign. It is the energy generated by the campaign—the efforts of a broad network of stakeholders in the nonprofit working together, pulling in the same direction—that makes the campaign such a good structure for raising bigger and better gifts.

LIVE & LEARN

The Wily Donor

The largest annual donor to a prominent museum was in very ill health. The director asked him to endow his gift before he passed away, that is, to create an endowment of a size that would produce the same level of annual income to the museum as his annual gift.

To support these efforts, the staff and trustees mounted an elaborate dinner to celebrate the donor's lifetime of generosity, even carrying him into the event on a splendidly decorated chair. He was thrilled with all the accolades and agreed to meet with the director to discuss the gift.

"I'm sorry, I've decided not to give you the endowment after all," he told the stunned director. "Instead, I've created a trust in my will that will give income to the program for the next 10 years." "But don't you want to see the benefits of your gift while you are still with us?" cried the disappointed director. "Well," said the donor, "I'm afraid if I give it all to you now, you won't pay any more attention to me."

Megagifts: A Whole New World

Big gifts have become more common in the past decade. As wealth increases, the number of millionaires goes up, and the incentives to give (whether personal or financial) become more attractive to higher-level donors, the gifts at the top of the philanthropic pyramid are becoming larger and larger. The number of gifts to nonprofits that exceed $20 million is now up to 100 per year, according to *The Chronicle of Philanthropy*.

The new megadonors are not like the philanthropists of an earlier era. A generation of dot-com entrepreneurs, many of them younger than the major donors of earlier decades, has set a new tone of engagement and involvement in the charitable organizations they support. Accountability, sophistication in financial investments, transparency of governance, and providing measurable outcomes have all come into play with the advent of larger gifts.

How Big Is Big?

The largest gifts, from individuals as well as huge national foundations like Gates or Annenberg, are now well into the hundreds of millions annually. Ted Turner's gift to the United Nations was a cool billion. Many donors, as well as some organizations, now view $1 million as an "entry-level" gift into the big time for players in the upper echelon of philanthropy. Gifts or bequests of $20 to $50 million to bring a new cause into the limelight are now relatively common, and more are announced monthly.

One way to look at the rise of the megagift is that nonprofits are doing a better job of cultivating and motivating donors. The entire spectrum of philanthropy—from identification of prospects to recognition pricing—has become much more sophisticated. Donors are seeing opportunities for making change, making an impact, and making their name stand out in a field that allows everyone involved to feel better about their actions. Nonprofits are improving their marketing and their solicitation techniques, and giving more attention to the relationships that lead to bigger gifts.

Numerous movements have been started in philanthropic circles to focus large gifts on support for specific needs. Solving the AIDS problem in Africa has attracted large grants and a whole new way of building infrastructure into third-world healthcare solutions, led by the Gates Foundation. Fixing the problems of big-city public schools has been a national priority, with foundations like Annenberg leading research and contributing resources to create new models. Funds targeting cancer and other specific diseases have enrolled the support of celebrity names, from Lance Armstrong to Christopher Reeve. Hurricanes, tsunamis, and earthquakes have elicited a tremendous outpouring of support, both big and little, to alleviate suffering.

Donors have seen that larger gifts make more of an impact, because more can be done with more resources. The private sector, from foundations to corporations to wealthy individuals, has made a huge commitment to solving the problems of the world, often going above and beyond the efforts of local, state, and national governments. The basic arguments for private philanthropy—to alleviate hardship, to make the world a better place to live in, to have impact, and to create change—have taken a major step forward with the advent of megagifts.

Prospecting for the Big Gift

The place to start is to find a donor with the resources to make a very large gift (see Exhibit 8.6). No organization receives a gift of $10 million from a donor with $5 million in assets. Look for a donor who is ready to give from assets, not just from income. Most people give away less than 5% of their income to charity on an annual basis; this means that to give away $10 million from income, the donor must earn $200 million, which is an unlikely scenario, even for the superrich. Most megagifts from individuals are made from assets, not from income.

EXHIBIT 8.6

Ways to Find Potential Megadonors

- Research who among your supporters sits on corporate boards and how much stock they own in the company.

- Watch for who in your constituency is selling a company, especially a family business.

- Learn who owns or develops large pieces of real estate in your region.

- With your board and leadership, review names of individuals of wealth who give to your cause.

- Keep track of large corporate and foundation gifts in your field.

- Stay abreast of local buyouts and research the national companies that come into your markets.

- Look for connections to national corporations and individuals of wealth among your vendors, including banks, insurance companies, investment firms, and other professional service providers.

- Read *The Wall Street Journal* to stay on top of business news; in its Weekend Edition every Friday, the *Journal* publishes a section on philanthropy that features donors of large gifts.

- Read *The Chronicle of Philanthropy* to learn about large donors and new gifts in your field; the *Chronicle* devotes one issue a year and many additional articles to profiling megadonors and their charitable interests.

RULES OF THE ROAD

Donor Honor Roll: The Competition's Prospect List

Assets come in a variety of forms. The research on your current donors and prospects should help you learn what kind of assets might be available for megagift giving. Use an electronic research tool to search for large stockholders in your current donor base to identify potential megadonors. Watch the business news and keep track of sales of family-owned businesses and entrepreneurial activities among your supporters. Learn about planned giving tools and educate your staff and volunteers on how to approach donors using them.

Other megagifts come from foundations or corporations that have a particular interest in the focus or service provided by your nonprofit. Become familiar with the foundation search tools and keep abreast of large gifts made to other organizations that do work in the same field as yours. Networking is a wonderful tool for finding hints about potential megadonors; talk to peers, attend professional meetings, keep up with other advancement professionals, and stay involved in your field to stay up to date with information on megadonations, giving patterns, and the interest areas of well-known donors.

Do not ignore the contacts and friendships with potential megagift donors that might exist already among members of your board and constituencies. Ask all board members to work with you on prospect identification. Review lists for colleagues whom your volunteers might know from other boards and charitable entities that they are involved with. Review business links, such as national suppliers to local corporations, and national investors in local business enterprises. Talk to local bankers, stockbrokers, and investment advisors. Your goal is to learn who has made great wealth, who has invested great wealth, and who among your constituents knows people of great wealth to whom they can introduce you.

Planning for Megagifts

Megagifts require both creativity and rigorous planning by the institution's leadership to be sold to the donor, integrated into the needs and mission of the nonprofit, and successfully implemented. Some nonprofits with large potential gifts have found that the gift takes them off-mission, into doing something they don't want to do. Others have found that new donors shy away from giving to them after a megagift has been announced, thinking that the nonprofit doesn't need any more money. All of the possible consequences require thoughtful analysis at the highest levels of the nonprofit, from the chief executive to the board chair.

Use creativity to spark the donor's imagination:

- What will really get her excited?

- What about the gift and its use will make things different?

- What impact will the gift have on the problem being addressed?

- How will the gift be announced and recognized?

- What kind of involvement will the donor have in the implementation and use of her gift?

But careful financial and strategic planning is required to make sure that the gift will do what the donor wants it to do:

- Does the organization have the knowledge, expertise, and human resources to deliver on what is promised?

- Does this gift fit into the organization's mission and objectives?

- What will it cost? Does this gift cover all the costs?

- Will it provide leverage? Is there a way to use this gift to encourage other donors to give to this purpose?

Megagifts also take time. Although there have been a few well-publicized cases where a donor approached for the first time by a nonprofit is completely swept away by their passionate presentation and commits to a gift of millions on the spot,

The Dot-com Billionaire

The engineering school of a major university proudly claimed one of the wealthiest of the Silicon Valley entrepreneurs as their alum. When he was in school, however, the guy had been a classic geek, sitting in the front row of every class and earning straight A's. He had been famous among his professors for being unable to speak up, not even able to ask a question in front of others. When offered the honor of giving the graduation speech as valedictorian, he had refused, citing his inability to speak in front of a crowd. The dean kindly agreed to appoint another speaker, thus sparing the young man untold embarrassment.

Now, 12 years later, the university president flew to California to ask the billionaire for a large gift to help kick off the public phase of the big engineering school capital campaign. "What would you think about giving us our first gift of $50 million?" the eager president asked.

The young man, still in his early 30s, hesitated to meet the president's gaze. He was wearing the typical West Coast uniform—a rumpled T-shirt, jeans, and tennis shoes. "Would I have to give a speech?" he finally mumbled, looking into the corner of the room. The president assured him the gift would be speech-free, and the deal was struck for $50 million.

these occasions are not the norm. Most donors of large gifts know the organization they are giving to, many have served on the board, and all are familiar with the good work that the nonprofit does in their field of service. Sometimes megagifts take decades, as the donor develops from a young annual supporter to a middle-aged major gift contributor to a megagift donor at the end of his lifetime. Patience is a virtue in development, where lifetime relationships produce lifetime gifts.

Asking for megagifts can be daunting. Sometimes development staff members are afraid to broach large numbers with donors because, if they get turned down, it means a great disappointment for the institution. Not surprisingly, blame can begin to fester and fingers are pointed when large numbers are at stake. The more vulnerable development staff member might want to invite a "heavyweight" solicitor, such as the board chair or the executive director, to accompany him on such a call. As in any major solicitation, the strongest approach comes from the member of the team who has the best relationship with the donor.

The critical key to bringing in a megagift is to ask—forthrightly, directly, and with facts and plans in hand. Very few donors will make an initial offer of a gift of millions, and donors who have enough assets to give away $50 or $100 million are not fools. They will ask hard questions and will expect hard answers. Be prepared to discuss the big picture, because this is a big-picture gift: Talk about the organization's future, its strategic initiatives, its priorities, its finances, its governance, its programs, and its potential.

The Best of the Rest

Asks for big gifts—those that are over $1 or $2 million—are not always successful, but just the act of making an ask for a megagift can position the rest of the organization for success in fundraising in major gifts. Asking for gifts of $5, $10, and even $50 million indicates that the nonprofit has big ideas. Big vision is almost always an asset in fundraising, because many successful businesspeople and entrepreneurs pride themselves on exhibiting this same quality. Of course, the institution needs to have the planning and capacity to back up the vision, but for some organizations, the situation becomes circular: Seeking $25 million is a way of "getting on the map" with the largest donors, those who have the capacity to give $25 million.

"Asking for too much" is therefore almost an oxymoron. Donors seldom are insulted at the assumption that they can make a large gift. Asking at the megalevel also brings up the expectations and can raise the gift levels of other donors who are involved in the solicitation. (This can include board members and volunteers who are simply informed about the pending meeting.) If one were to be strategic, for instance, one could set up a solicitation for $10 million with an ancillary goal of cultivating and raising the sights of the volunteer solicitor, if she herself is capable of a gift of that size. This is a means of using a solicitation to raise the sights of the solicitor, not just the one being solicited.

To explore another possible outcome, a donor who is asked for a gift of $10 million might respond that that is much too high, but be swayed by the high ask amount into giving $1 million as a fallback position. Later he admits that he was really planning to give only $500,000, so the institution doubled its gift size by making an ask on the high side of what was deemed possible. "Asking for too much" thus can be a technique to raise gifts that are larger than the institution had expected from specific donors.

There is a danger that if the megagift is realized, other donors will feel that their funds are not necessary for the success of the institution. Hospitals and universities that have received gifts of $100 million and more have learned ways to counter this problem. One technique is to create a campaign and a table of needs that identifies the megagift as the leadership gift, then develop a gift table that will require much more in giving at lower levels to reach success. Another option is to create and market attractive giving options at the $1 to $5 million level, below the megagift, that will still attract key donors and build a strong major gift fundraising program.

The terms of the megagift itself might assist in making a strong case for other gifts; identifying a portion of the large gift as a match, for instance, might help leverage new gifts or bring in bigger gifts from previous donors. Finally, some megagifts that are planned gifts or that go into endowments really won't have a big impact right away on the institutional needs and programs. An effort must be made to explain the long-term nature of the impact to other donors when the big gift is announced.

Summary

Special interest areas in major gifts can reveal additional techniques, tools, and strategies for raising large gifts. Planned gifts, for instance, can be integrated into a major gift program through training of staff and volunteers in the basic tools and techniques associated with gifts that are not cash or pledges. These gifts can pay back an enormous amount to the nonprofit over time. Although some require substantial expertise, others are easy to use, and all of them can be a part of the package of tools used when soliciting a major donor.

Capital campaigns also provide an array of techniques and supporting tools for use when soliciting major gifts. The excitement, marketing support, and momentum that accrue to a well-planned capital campaign can attract donors who might not otherwise have considered a major gift to your organization. The judicious use of campaign planning tools, such as gift tables, tables of need, and feasibility studies, also can help major gift prospects understand the nonprofit's needs and case, and enable them to have input in the planning phase in ways that encourage them to give more.

Finally, the megagift has arrived in the philanthropic world. Big gifts of $50, $100, and $200 million are setting a new bar for leadership-level donations. Finding the right donor, planning the right gift, and working to ensure that the gift actually will help the institution meet its goals are all factors that need to be assessed in working with gifts at this level. The possibility of making a great impact with a huge gift is tremendously attractive to both nonprofits and to donors, and can become one element—a leading element—of the successful major gift program.

Case Studies in Major Gifts

Case Study I: Starting from Zero in Major Gifts

The Story

Steps to Ownership was a small, grassroots housing nonprofit that wanted to raise $500,000 for a new home ownership center. Its mission: to help low-income families learn how to buy and pay for a home of their own. The nonprofit offered training and support on every component of the process, from saving money for the down payment to applying for a low-interest mortgage. Much of the work was done by volunteers, with a paid staff of five providing training and organizational support. Staff salaries, training materials, and housing seminars were supported by federal grants and some local public funds available through the mayor's office of housing.

Steps to Ownership had been incorporated as a nonprofit eight years earlier and was still run by its founding director, an articulate and well-educated African American woman with a background in minority banking, who was committed to improving the lives of impoverished families. Her organization could show real achievements, with hundreds of minority families now participating in the American dream of owning their own home. She could point to entire blocks of urban homes—formerly in terrible disrepair—that had been restored and brought back into the housing stock through private ownership.

The nonprofit's board was made up of community advocates, minority home owners who had made use of their services, and a few devoted teachers and volunteers. They were caring and intelligent people, but they were not people of wealth. Their experience in fundraising was limited to running an annual street fair, which netted approximately $10,000 per year.

Their community relationships were not fully developed. They had received some advice and support from the urban studies program of their local university, and some university students volunteered to help in their training programs. The director served on the board of the regional community foundation. With almost no resources, the nonprofit was about to take on its first major gifts effort. It had no advancement staff, no previous donors, no board members of wealth, and no volunteers with major gift fundraising experience. How should they proceed?

Questions to Consider

- How should the organization determine how much money it needs to raise?

- Who should it hire to help raise money?

- How can the nonprofit identify and recruit volunteers with experience?

- How should the campaign be organized?

- What is the nonprofit's case and what materials are needed?

- Who should lead the campaign?

- How should the nonprofit pay for the campaign?

- What can it do to identify prospects? Who are the prospects?

- How should the nonprofit cultivate and solicit prospects?

- How should new donors be thanked and recognized?

- Is there a way to position the drive so that new donors can be encouraged to stay involved with the organization?

- What will be the long-term effects of the campaign on the organization?

What Actually Happened

Defining the Need

The need for a new housing center was readily apparent. The client base had grown well beyond the numbers that could be comfortably dealt with in their current office, a space of no more than a few cubicles in a run-down building sandwiched between a laundry and a bar. Paint was peeling off the walls and there was no privacy for personal financial discussions. The nonprofit needed office space in the neighborhood, near clients, that was clean, well-lit, safe, and appropriate for the work. Besides, the nonprofit had lost its lease and would have to move one way or another.

One board member called on a friend, an architect who had an interest in urban planning. (He eventually became so involved in the organization that he joined the board.) The architect donated his time to identify a building in disrepair that could be bought and renovated on a main street in their neighborhood. He also donated his expertise (using support from student interns) to design the space, create floor plans, and even drew a colored rendering for use with potential donors. The total project was priced out at $500,000, which became the goal for the campaign.

Identifying Professional Support

It was clear to everyone involved that professional fundraising help was needed. The director felt she had two choices: Hire a staff development officer or bring in a consultant to provide support for the campaign. She didn't have a source of funding identified to pay an expensive consultant, but she wasn't sure that she could afford to pay a development staff member after the capital campaign was over. In addition, she wanted someone with experience who could hit the ground running, rather than a staff member who would grow with the organization.

The group decided to draw on the expertise of someone already familiar with campaigns and agreed to hire a campaign consultant. They applied to the community foundation and received a capacity building grant to pay the consultant's fees. The community foundation director had worked with several consultants involved with other projects and recommended two. After interviews and extended discussions, the board members made their choice. The consultant was hired and began to draw up a campaign plan.

The Planning Phase

The consultant created a campaign plan, a gift table, naming opportunities, and a timetable for the drive. She then focused on bringing in volunteers with fundraising capacity and experience. First, she suggested the names of several people who could be helpful on the board; they included a banker, a mortgage company representative, a community activist, and a trustee of a family foundation who was sympathetic to the cause. Next, she helped the organization create a new Building Committee, made up of several current board members and several new potential donors who had supported minority programs in other parts of the city.

The consultant's next goal was to work on the case. Working closely with the director and national resources like Fannie Mae, she found that the case for home ownership is a strong one. Owning one's home has become an important step in building communities. Home equity has been identified as a source of building wealth for families over decades, helping to move many poor and immigrant families into the middle class. Children who grow up in homes that are owned by their parents are less likely to turn to crime, drop out of school, and become teenage parents.

The consultant and the director wrote a simple four-page brochure that featured the importance of home ownership in building minority communities. It told the personal stories of several graduates of the Steps to Ownership program. The brochure also included pictures of the home owners, their renovated homes, and the neighborhood improvements. The consultant developed a packet including the brochure, a fact sheet about the program, copies of two articles from national journals on home ownership, and the naming options available in the new center. The entire packet (except for the brochure) was printed on a desktop computer. All of it fit into a stock glossy folder bought at an office supply store.

The consultant drew up an initial prospect list, which was augmented by the board and Building Committee members. It was made up of local foundations interested in community issues, local companies with employees who were graduates of the program, and a few wealthy individuals whose homes bordered the neighborhood that was undergoing revitalization. The consultant then provided fundraising training for the members of the Building Committee.

Recruiting Volunteer Leadership

The consultant, the director, and the committee spent a great deal of time deciding whom to ask to chair the Building Committee. Finally they settled on the president of a local bank who they knew was interested in building a client base in the minority community. The director, accompanied by a board member who had ties to the bank, made the call to recruit the banker. After some discussion about staffing and support issues (to be provided by the consultant), the president agreed. They were on their way!

Implementation: Raising Major Gifts

The chairman and his committee felt that the nonprofit was not well known enough to prospective donors to make calls without some level of prior cultivation. They planned a small cultivation event, a late-afternoon reception and meeting. The event featured brief presentations by three of the housing program graduates, who all talked movingly about their experiences. The event was hosted in the bank's boardroom, which was provided free of charge, and it was well attended. Those who came were told the organization's story and asked to help. No money was asked for at the cultivation event.

The Building Committee also invited prospective donors to tour the neighborhood where the organization's work was focused, bringing prospects into the homes of several graduates of the housing program. Not all the prospects on the original list attended the cultivation events, but about 25 attended either the reception or the tour. The committee agreed to focus its efforts on this group of 25 "likely" prospects.

Calls were assigned to members of the Building Committee, packets prepared, and the solicitations began. All of the likely prospects were rated at the level of $10,000 to $50,000. The consultant prepared a proposal template for the foundations, which were visited personally by the committee chair. Because the prospect group had already been made familiar with the program and the need, the volunteers quickly found that if an appointment was accepted, a gift was forthcoming. Not all donors gave at the level they had been rated, but an initial foundation pledge of $50,000 helped to anchor the campaign, and the pledges began to come in.

Several volunteers had difficulty asking for money. The consultant paired them with others who were more experienced or joined the calls herself. The director polished her own fundraising skills by accompanying the bank president on calls. The star of the committee was the president of the bank, who made every call rated at the level of $25,000 and up—a total of eight calls—and personally raised over half of the money. His leadership was the key to the success of the campaign, although several unexpected bumps in the road caused trouble along the way.

Unexpected Problems that Arose During the Drive

- The cost estimate for the new center was $100,000 too low.

- A competing organization with a similar mission launched a campaign at the same time Steps to Ownership did.

The consultant, the director, and the committee chairman dealt with the difficulties as they arose. When the cost estimate went up because of problems encountered in the building renovation, they decided that more funds had to be raised (rather than cutting back, which was another option available). Additional prospects were needed to meet the new goal, and the extra $100,000 proved to be difficult to raise. The initial timetable was six months; the extra 20% increase to the goal cost the group another three months of fundraising.

The competing organization beat the group to several of the local foundations, costing them some initial gifts. During the cultivation process, however, the chairman was able to bring the foundation people back for a tour of the neighborhood. The work that had been done on the homes was so impressive that the funders came through in the next funding cycle with grants.

Recognition and Stewardship

The donors were all invited to a neighborhood celebration dedicating the new home ownership center. A local restaurant donated food. Gifts made were recognized by a printed sign and a handout with names of the donors. The mayor and his housing office director gave speeches. The organization, its clients, and its new donors were all ecstatic over the beautiful new building.

Months later, the nonprofit's annual report was sent to the donors with a report updating on the work of the center. The director's goal to turn all the building donors into annual donors was not met. Many of the donors were more interested in a one-time capital gift than in an ongoing commitment to the organization's operating budget. Some long-term relationships that benefited the nonprofit in the long run were developed, however.

Long-term Results

Two years later, Steps to Ownership had a stronger board, an active development committee, and had just hired a young and committed full-time development officer. Several of the local foundations were still making grants, and one had a staff member who was now on the nonprofit's board. The president of the bank had also asked a bank staff member to join the board. The organization was in its new home, significantly stronger, and in a better position to raise more funds to meet its goals.

Fundraising Costs

- The nonprofit had to pay costs of $3,500. This was paid out of the non-profit's operating budget. The costs represented an overhead of less than 1% of the $600,000 raised. Even with the consultant's fees included, the total cost of $28,500 represented a little less than 5% of the funds raised, a very reasonable amount for cost of funds raised. By anyone's measure, this was a very efficient campaign.

- Consultant's fees: $25,000, paid for by a grant from the community foundation.

- Materials: $3,000 for the brochure; $500 for folders, paper, materials, signage, and the invitation and mailing costs for the cultivation events.

- Event costs: all donated.

- Architect's fees: donated.

Funds Raised

- Steps to Ownership raised the entire $600,000 goal to build its new center in nine months.

Case Study II: Building Major Gifts Capacity After a False Start

The Story

A small museum, the Museum of Contemporary Arts, planned to raise money for several pressing needs. Although it was 20 years old, it had only a tiny endowment of $1.5 million. Many of its peers had much larger endowments. The board also wanted to raise money for technology and educational programs to help improve ties in the community, which was a core part of the museum's mission. Finally, a local art collector had promised to donate his entire collection of American twentieth-century paintings if the museum could build a new wing to house them.

The museum had an active board, including younger members of several of the older, wealthy, philanthropic families in the city. The board chairman was a real go-getter, an entrepreneur who had great vision for where the museum should go but little experience gathering consensus and building support for how to get there. The director was new, from out of town, and not yet familiar with the local fundraising scene. There was a membership director and a grants writer on staff, but neither had run a campaign or a major gifts effort.

The community relationships were beginning to bear fruit. The city had an active arts scene, and the museum coordinated an event called Art Nights Out once a month with two other museums close by. In addition, the museum had begun to invite middle and high school art teachers to regular seminars and workshops, conducted with a grant received from a local foundation.

The board was eager to get started and raise the money. Members felt that many of the local corporations would support them, because the museum attracted tourists to the region, and the local economy was highly tourist dependent. They created a Campaign Committee, declared a goal of $10 million, placed the board chair in charge, and went out to raise the money.

After six months, they had raised exactly $75,000. None of the initial companies they had targeted had made gifts. The board members were burned out and discouraged. Many felt let down by the chairman, who had not made his own gift. The new director wasn't sure why the campaign had failed and began to think that he had landed in a community that wasn't prepared to support the arts. What to do now?

Questions to Consider

- How should the organization decide what its priorities are and how much money it needs to raise?

- Who should it hire to help raise money?

- How should the campaign be organized?

- How can the organization get its board members to make their own gifts?

- What is the museum's case and what materials are needed?

- Who should lead the fundraising effort?

- How should the museum pay for the cost of fundraising?

- What can it do to identify prospects? Who are the museum's prospects?

- How should prospects be cultivated and solicited?

- How should donors be thanked and recognized?

- Is there a way to position the drive so that new donors can be encouraged to stay involved with the organization?

- What will be the drive's long-term effect on the organization?

What Actually Happened

Defining the Need

The museum director decided to step back and take a broader look at the plans for the future of the museum. He and the board chair agreed to temporarily freeze the campaign in order to create a long-term strategic plan. With a new board strategic planning committee in place, the vision began to take shape; in six months, group members had a well-documented set of needs that matched their mission and goals. They spent the time and effort to build support from board members for the plan, a key level of engagement that had been missing in their previous attempt, which had been spearheaded by the chairman with little input from anyone else.

The fundraising plan based on the new needs totaled $12 million, even more than the original effort had aimed for. There were three components: the plan called for raising $6 million in endowment, $3 million in program costs, and $3 million for capital construction of the new wing. The plan was ambitious, but they were sure that the funds could be raised with an organized fundraising effort focused on major gifts from individuals and foundations interested in the arts. (The committee had given up on the city's corporate base after their last experience.)

Identifying Professional Support

The director met with the board development committee and asked for their assistance in doing a feasibility study. Two of the members, both second-generation art aficionados, agreed to ante up $25,000 each to pay for the study, which was conducted by a national fundraising firm with experience in the arts. The firm came in, reviewed the strategic plan components, and worked with the board to select 30 individuals to interview. They targeted 10 interviews with foundation people, 10 individuals, and 10 corporate executives in order to help the museum learn who their prospects really were. The entire study took another three months, with the results presented at a full board meeting.

Feasibility Study Results

The feasibility study proved very interesting. The interviews showed that the museum had the capacity to raise about $8 million, mostly from individuals and local foundations where the trustees were interested in the arts. Although there might be a few corporate donations, the consultants felt that the business donors in their community were focused heavily on K to 12 education. Maybe there was a niche there to help raise some educational program funds, but that would have to be explored further.

The study also delivered some opinions on the themes, or the case, that might deliver best for the campaign. The consultants recommended using two themes: the first would focus on education, tying the expanded educational programming at the museum to cuts in the local schools' arts programs; the second would focus on the economic development aspects of the museum and its success in marketing itself to visitors.

Finally, the study delivered some potential names for prospects, volunteers, and even a possible chairman for the drive if the museum wanted to expand the volunteer committee beyond current board members.

Board members were so pleased with the report that they agreed to hire the consulting firm to advise them on their campaign. For $3,000 a month, the consultant would fly in once a month to meet with the committee. The contract also included unlimited phone and e-mail access to the consultant in between visits. They planned to pay for the consultant out of campaign receipts.

The Planning Phase

The consultant helped the group strategize about their organization. They ultimately created a Campaign Committee that included both board members and some of the nonboard volunteers identified through the feasibility study. In a show of optimism, the board also declared that they would raise the full $12 million in identified needs, even though the study showed prospects for only $8 million in funding. They were sure that additional prospects would be identified throughout the campaign.

The consultant delivered a campaign plan, a timetable, a gift table, and recommended naming options with prices attached. He also convinced the board and the director that the time had come to hire a staff development director; he, the consultant, could provide ongoing advice and support, but it was important to have a dedicated staff person at the museum to coordinate the volunteer efforts, make calls, prepare materials, and support the campaign. A search was begun and an individual hired, with relatively little experience, at $55,000. With benefits included, the annual cost to the museum was almost $80,000.

With the help of their new director and the two staff members, the museum put together a 14-page full color campaign brochure. The piece was lovely and featured many of the artworks the museum had in its collection. It also focused on the two themes—education and economic development—that the feasibility study had identified. The back page listed all the naming options available for gifts at each level, ranging from $10,000 to $1,500,000 to name the new wing.

Prospect identification continued with the assistance of the entire team.

First, the consultant helped the museum to hire an electronic prospect screening firm to run the entire membership base through and identify individuals of wealth. Then the membership director, who was the person most familiar with the database and had strong computer skills, was trained as a prospect researcher. She researched information on individuals and foundations from several online sources that the museum invested in.

The consultant worked from the initial 30 feasibility study interviews to create a list of about 50 prospects; these were individuals and foundations that were identified as being interested in art and capable of a gift of $10,000 or more. The museum staff augmented the list from their electronic screening and prospect research results.

After the prospect list was developed, board members participated in a screening and rating session. They reviewed the list of names in a group setting, made some additions and deletions, and rated each prospect. The entire planning process took another three months, so it was a full year from the time the earlier fund drive was frozen to the point where they were ready to start fundraising again. Finally, they were off and running!

Recruiting Volunteer Leadership

The consultant felt strongly that the chairman of the board should not be the sole chair of the campaign. There were good reasons for this recommendation: The chair was now very busy with his new company; he had not been terribly successful in the earlier effort; and, as he would be involved in the fundraising anyway, it would be useful to broaden the reach of the committee by recruiting another leader to help with the "heavy lifting."

Given the consultant's advice, the executive committee of the board made an important decision: They decided to have three co-chairs run the campaign. They asked the chairman of the board to remain as one of the co-chairs, reaffirming his importance to their efforts. But they agreed to recruit two new leaders: a longtime donor to the arts in the community, who knew many of the older individuals and family foundation members, and a younger woman, socially well connected, who had led campaigns for several other nonprofits and was married to a wealthy developer. In this manner they expanded their prospect pool, tripled their outreach to prospects, and added energy and enthusiasm for their cause all in one step.

Implementation: Raising Major Gifts

The very first thing the consultant had the new leaders do was to solicit the other members of the board and make a gift themselves. This decision proved to be the key to the success of the entire campaign. The members of the board, having worked for a year to identify the needs, direct the feasibility study, plan the campaign, rate prospects, and identify the volunteer leadership, were now very committed to making the campaign work.

The three co-chairs were solicited first by the director. On the consultant's advice, he suggested that they make a pledge together to create a matching fund and challenge the rest of the board to reach that amount through the board's total giving. The director suggested the amount of $1.5 million from the three co-chairs, or $500,000 each. After some discussion about the matching rules and the pledge payout terms, all three co-chairs agreed to the plan.

Using the challenge, the co-chairs went to solicit their fellow board members. In only two months, they had over $3 million in additional pledges in hand. When the campaign volunteers began to move beyond the board to solicit individuals, corporations, and foundations in the community, they had already raised $4.5 million, or 37.5% of their goal. Raising the rest of the money turned out to be a relatively straightforward matter, once the board had made their own commitment clear for all to see.

Of course, it took a lot of work to raise the remaining funds. The committee decided to host a series of small group dinners at private homes to help cultivate the prospects on their list. They found that attractive, elegant events where they simply presented their case, without asking for money, worked well. They targeted each event to specific subsets of their prospect pool, with fewer than 10 couples at each home. The hosts paid for each of the events, which were staffed by the new development director.

The museum also put the skills of the grant writer on staff to good use, raising over $4 million from corporate and foundation sources for education programs. The naming gift of $1.5 million for the new wing was eventually secured from—to everyone's surprise—the man who had promised them his collection in the first place. And last, but not least, the chairman of the board, proud that his new business had at last taken off, came in at the end and pledged another $1 million to push the campaign beyond its goal, on top of his earlier $500,000 matching challenge gift.

Recognition and Stewardship

The campaign ended with the dedication and opening of the new wing. The donor of the art, the same person whose name now graced the exterior of the new wing, was feted at a huge ball. The co-chairs were given signed prints by a famous local artist; donors above $100,000 received tiny glass sculptures (designed by a local artist, of course). The list of donors at $10,000 and above was published and circulated to all museum members in the quarterly newsletter and mounted on a permanent brass plaque in the museum's central hall.

In addition, the museum's Web site was redesigned to include banners of the corporate supporters of the campaign. Each donor of $10,000 and more was given free membership for three years, along with two free tickets to the annual black-tie event. All donors received the museum's annual report for three years and were included in the mailing of the quarterly arts newsletter produced by the staff.

Long-term Results

The success of the campaign catapulted the museum into the top rung of social and cultural institutions of the region. Events were better attended, outreach efforts better received, and the number of new memberships rose (partly due to the effect of opening the new wing, which attracted considerable national attention).

Like many museums, however, they soon learned that operating costs had also increased. The museum had hired a development director, who stayed on the staff beyond the campaign. The board had—perhaps without clear foresight—given free membership and free event tickets to all their top donors, so fundraising event receipts were down.

The museum was not able to raise enough through new memberships and admissions to cover the ongoing costs of operating the new wing. It needed a new curator of American paintings and couldn't afford one. The new $5 million in endowment was invested at the end of the dot-com frenzy and didn't earn a great deal in the early years of the twenty-first century. *The museum had arrived—only to find that it was in dire need of more funds for operations.* (But that is a problem to be covered in another case study.)

Actual Costs

- Cost of the consultant: $3,000 per month for 3 years = $108,000, plus an additional $18,000 for consultant's travel expenses, plus the feasibility study of $50,000, which had been paid for by two board members. Total consulting fees: $176,000

- Cost of adding the development director: $80,000 × 3 years = $240,000

- Brochure: $15,000

- Cost of electronic screening and research capacity: $25,000

- Cultivation events and the dedication ball: donated

- Printing of invitations, donors lists, programs: $5,000

- Plaques, glass sculpture gifts, prints: $30,000

- Total costs for the campaign: $491,000, or about 3.3% of the funds raised (A very efficiently run campaign.)

Funds Raised

- The Museum of Contemporary Art raised $15 million, $3 million more than its goal, and $7 million more than the feasibility study showed could be raised, over a period of three years.

Index

C

E